Between Two Worlds

Between Two Worlds

The American Novel in the 1960's

by

Sanford Pinsker

The Whitston Publishing Company
Troy, New York
1980

Copyright 1980
Sanford Pinsker

ISBN 0-87875-169-6

Library of Congress Catalog Card Number 79-64168

Printed in the United States of America

Dedication

To the memory of my parents, who also lived between two worlds.

Contents

ACKNOWLEDGEMENTS

As always, Franklin & Marshall College was very generous in its support and my students were not shy about insisting upon clarity. I have learned to depend upon—and appreciate—both conditions.

Parts of the manuscript have appeared, in slightly altered form, in *Studies in the Twentieth Century, Southern Review, Barat Review, Critque* and *Connecticut Review.* I wish to thank the editors and publishers of these journals for permission to reprint.

Finally: I would like to thank the following publishers for permission to quote from the sources listed:

Alfred A. Knopf, Inc., for *The Dick* by Bruce Jay Friedman, copyright 1963; Candida Donadio Associates, Inc., for *Stern* by Bruce Jay Friedman, copyright 1963 and for *A Mother's Kisses* by Bruce Jay Friedman, copyright 1964; Crown Publishers, Inc., for *Cassandra Singing* by David Madden, © 1969 by David Madden; Delacorte Press/Seymour Lawrence, for *Cat's Cradle,* copyright 1963, *God Bless You, Mr. Rosewater,* copyright 1965, *Mother Night,* copyright 1961 and *Slaughterhouse-Five,* copyright 1969 by Kurt Vonnegut, Jr.; *Dissent* "Styron and His Black Critics" by Jervis Anderson, copyright 1969; Doubleday & Co., for *The Floating Opera,* copyright © 1956, 1967 and *Lost in the Funhouse,* copyright © 1968 by John Barth and for *Scoring* by Dan Greenburg, copyright © 1972 by Dan Greenburg; E. P. Dutton for *After the Tradition: Essays on Modern Jewish Writing* by Robert Alter, copyright © 1969, 1968, 1967, 1966, 1965, 1964, 1962, 1961 by Robert Alter; Farrar, Straus & Giroux, Inc., for *The Fixer* by Bernard Malamud, copyright © 1966 by Bernard Malamud, for *A Crown of Feathers,* copyright © 1970, 1971, 1972, 1973, *A Friend of Kafka and Other Stories,* copyright © 1962, 1966, 1967, 1968, 1969, 1970, *The Seance,* copyright © 1964, 1965, 1966, 1967, 1968 and *Short Friday,* copyright © 1961, 1962, 1963, 1964 by Isaac Bashevis Singer; Houghton Mifflin Company for *Goodbye, Columbus* by Philip Roth, copyright 1967; John Barth for "The Literature of Exhaustion" by John Barth, copyright 1967 by the author's agent, Lurton Blassingame; *New York Times* for "The Irrevocable Reputation," by Anatole Broyard, © 1971 by the New York Times Company; New York University Press for *Isaac Bashevis Singer and the Eternal Past* by Irving Buchen, copyright 1968; Partisan Review for "Gimpel, the Fool" by Isaac Bashevis Singer, copyright May-June, 1953, by *Partisan Review; Playboy* for "Cross the Border, Close the Gap" by Leslie Fiedler,

I

An Introduction of Sorts

> "*Wandering between two worlds, one dead,*
> *The other powerless to be born.   . .*"
>
> —*Matthew Arnold.*

Matthew Arnold must seem a strange choice indeed to pre-
face a study on the American novel in the 1960's. The prophetic
voice ought, by rights, to be Leslie Fiedler's. After all, it was
Fiedler who announced not only the death of Modernism, but the
curious birth of what we have agreed, for lack of a better term,
to call Post-Modernism. As he gleefully put it (in the pages of
Playboy magazine, no less);

> Almost all living readers and writers are aware of a fact which
> they have no adequate words to express, not in English certainly, nor
> even in American. We are living, have been living for two decades—and
> have been acutely conscious of the fact since 1955—through the death
> throes of Modernism and the birth pangs of Post-Modernism. The kind
> of literature which had arrogated to itself the name Modern (with the
> presumption that it represented the ultimate advance in sensibility and
> form, that beyond it newness was not possible), and whose moment of
> triumph lasted from a point just before World War I until one just after
> World War II, is *dead,* i.e. belongs to history, not actuality In the field
> of the novel, this means that the age of Proust, Mann, and Joyce is over;
> just as in verse that of T.S. Eliot, Paul Valery, Montale and Seferis is
> done with. [1]

To be sure, invitations to attend the burial of the novel had been
extended for some time--and, one might add, without doing much
damage to either the writers who continued to produce novels or

the readers who continued to read them. But what Fiedler felt compelled to announce was an obituary which foreclosed the possibility of eloquent elegies in advance. The contemporary moment, for Fiedler at least, could be characterized as "apocalyptic, anti-rational, blatantly romantic and sentimental"; its sacred texts were Westerns (e.g. Thomas Berger's *Little Big Man),* science fiction (e.g. Kurt Vonnegut's *Sirens Of Titan)* and pornography (Hubert Selby's *Last Exit To Brooklyn*), although not necessarily in that order and without that sense of critical discrimination which had been such a preoccupation with the Modernists. No! (in yet another thunder), this was "an age dedicated to joyous misology and prophetic irresponsibility"—a time that the late Richard Hofstadter (in that other critical country called Columbia) had planned to write about as *The Age Of Garbage.*

Fiedler, of course, was not alone. The high-priestess of anti-Art, Susan Sontag, added some wrinkles of her own (in *Against Interpretation*) and, soon, the "good news" made the rounds via that grape vine Ma Bell can neither charge for nor tap. And the Annuciation was this: novels, if they tried less, could become a Campbell's soup can. And for those with suspicions (albeit Modernist ones) that all this frenzy to lower—or demo'.sh—standards smacked of a philistinism we had heard before, there was Louis Kampf and his steady reassurances that the battle lines involved populism (newly defined as the "people" to whom all power should rightfully flow) vs. elitists of every stripe, including the literary. Modernist literature quickly became a convenient whipping boy in a scenerio filled with Hobson's choices about high-brow culture or wide-scale relevance.[2] That I have buried his tedious argumentation in the relative obscurity of a footnote is probably more dignity than such a position deserves.

However, *all* critics of contemporary literature (including the one you are now reading) are victims of that wonderful itch known as the prophetic urge. Long before the cunning of history has sifted through the canon and made the sorts of judgments blessed by hindsight, the working critic has already played his hunches out in print. It is the difference between receiving opinions and helping to form them, between life in the cool darkness of library stacks and life at the hot center. The latter has an almost Byronic attraction, but it has built-in dangers as well. It is never easy to know which writers stand at the vital crossroads, especially when so many signboards (neon or otherwise) announce the hottest product, the latest gesture, the newest gimmick. Fashion, after all, is a Protean commodity, formed as much by academic critics as their journalistic counterparts. And, in the Sixties, the two camps were nearly indistinguishable. Reputations were created in something like a direct proportion to academic interest in a Post-Modern spirit that stubbornly refused to show its face. T.S. Eliot once claimed that all a literary critic needed was intelligence; in the sheer welter of stuff being written about contemporary literature, an electric typewriter and air mail stamps might be more to the point.

For all of these reasons—and some which remain merely idiosyncratic—the essays which follow avoid that thread-like thesis a reader might follow through the labyrinth of contemporary literature. As Moses Herzog points out, with not a little wryness: "What this country needs is a good five cent synthesis." Post-Modernists could use one too, even if it had a thread-bare look on reflection. But I have decided to approach the problem from an oblique angle, one which will consider some central preoccupations (black humor, the gothic temper, reflexive preoccupations, etc.) of some centrally important writers (Bruce Jay Friedman, Joyce Carol Oates, John Barth). Nothing—with the possible exception of metaphysical rumination—is more boring than apologies in advance. As long as one first clears the air with "confession," everything from the tasteless to the wrong-headed will, presumably, be forgiven. It is a lesson we have learned from Norman Podhoretz (*Making It*) and a host of poets out to tell us the gory details of busted marriages or cracking up.

And yet, one owes his favorite writers *something*, especially if his study catches them in mid-career. After all, an arbitrary division like "the Sixties" is likely to mean more to critics than working artists. That Thomas Pynchon's *The Crying of Lot 49* (1966) rates a mention while *Gravity's Rainbow* (1973) is overlooked seems patently absurd, except in the curious world in which a critic actually writes. Books always "in-progress," continually up-dating themselves in the light of even newer novels, have notoriously bad track records where the nasty facts of publication are concerned. Granted, the impulse for comprehensiveness, like that for "perfection," would make for fewer critical books, but not necessarily better ones. The sad fact is that the very bulk of critical commentary is what makes the best sort of hindsight possible.

The epigraph from Arnold which gives this volume its title seemed a perfect way to summarize the situation. And too, as the speaker in "Stanzas From the Grand Chartreuse" laments the passing of that faith which finds its last adherents in an isolated monastery, analogies spring to mind in ways my former teachers would never have approved. Yet, the sort of devotion Arnold is half-writing an eloquent obituary about bears a strong relationship to the Formalistic love expended on behalf of sacred texts like *Ulysses* or *The Waste Land.* There is a sense, of course, in which *all* writers imagine themselves caught between "two worlds, one dead [i.e. established and nearly always hostile to the *new*]/The other powerless to be born. . .," but contemporary novelists felt it more keenly. The very writers they had studied as under-graduates (and, often, in graduate seminars as well) were presences who made it hard to presume, much less to begin. Hand-wringing about literary possibilities used up—or, as John Barth put it, "ex-hausted"—became a preoccupation in its own right. Others had more success where the past was concerned, particularly if they hit upon ways to dismiss it out of hand. In short, what follows are strategies toward a definition of what it means to live and write in a Post-Modernist world. Some of the directions are tentatively put, with visions still very much in search of themselves. Others come on with a hairy-chested certainty which stamps them as distinctly "American."

If the last group sounds like avatars of Ernest Hemingway, the relationship to characters living or dead is more than coinci-dence. It was Hemingway who had sounded the death knell for the outworn language of an outmoded age: "Abstract words such as glory, honor, courage, or hallow were obscene beside the concrete names of villages, the numbers of roads, the names of rivers, the numbers of regiments and the dates." *A Farewell To Arms* (1929) provided a manifesto for hard-boiled postures. In the novels which followed, would-be tough guys filled in his framework with the appropriate monosyllables. It had an "American" ring, which is to say, a gutsy, go-for-broke attitude all its own. And if Nick Adams (whose last name is, in effect, the signature of *every* American protagonist) or Jake Barnes or Robert Jordan often turned up with a romantic, even mushy, heart, so much the better. To be sure, the much-imitated Hemingway style was deceptive. His attitudes may have been Populist, easily transported to popular culture via Humphrey Bogart or Dashiell Hammett, but his literary grounding was thoroughly Modernist, full of those ironic brushstrokes and mythic substructures we associate with the higher brows of Joyce or Mann.

It is perhaps poetic justice that literary sons repay their paternal influences with the only coin they know—an Oedipal onslaught against those very victories older writers had shored against their ruin. The scenerio is familiar enough: sons replace fathers only to, later, be replaced by *their* sons. Ironically enough, it is the sort of cycle Hemingway himself had applied with such dazzling brilliance to the world of prizefighters. But in 1944 Saul Bellow turned the literary tables, directing his attack against the very ground conditions which had made a Hemingway seem so unique:

> Most serious matters are closed to the hardboiled. They are unpractised in introspection, and therefore badly equipped to deal with opponents whom they cannot shoot like big game or outdo in daring.[3]

The book was *Dangling Man* and in its peculiar geography of what Bellow called "the craters of the spirit," the novel not only introduced a likely candidate to succeed the likes of Hemingway, Fitzgerald and Faulkner, but provided the American Fifties with a convenient metaphor as well.

This is not to suggest that *machismo*, American-style disappeared as easily as those "abstract words" Hemingway abandoned in the grim realities of World War I. Like Capital-I Innocence, the two-fisted American Hero who confronts terrible whales (Ahab) or a timeless West (Natty Bumppo & Co.) could still look forward to a long run in the country's imagination. Norman Mailer, for example, raised the good orgasm to heights that would have embarrassed even a Hemingway. The earth had a sexy way of moving in *For Whom the Bell Tolls;* with Mailer, the political dialectics of, say, *The Naked and the Dead* (1948) degenerated into the sexual fireworks of *An American Dream* (1965).

But for all the residue of belief in the gun battle at high noon, the mythic fish or bear which teases us into initiation, the

sheer complexity of American life made such metaphors seem hopelessly outmoded. With sophisticated missles flying overhead, there
was not much point to sitting on the curb, playing poker and swapping lies about whores. Saul Bellow was perhaps the first American
novelist since Henry James who did not avoid, out of principle,
applying raw intelligence to the contemporary situation. And yet,
for all the idea-jousting in Moses Herzog's "mental letters" or
Arthur Sammler's meditative reflections on such neo-Romantic
phenomena as "spontaneity" or "freedom," it is faith affirmed,
rather than Ideas synthesized, which remains his strongest suit.
As Sammler puts it:

> You had to be a crank to insist on being right. Being right was largely
> a matter of explanations. Intellectual man had become an explaining
> creature. Fathers to children, wives to husbands, lecturers to listeners,
> experts to laymen, colleagues to colleagues, doctors to patients, man
> to his own soul explained. The roots of this, the causes of the other,
> the sources of events, the history, the structure, the reasons why.
> For the most part, in one ear and out the other. The soul wanted what
> it wanted. It had its own natural knowledge. It sat unhappily on super-
> structure of explanation, poor bird, not knowing which way to fly.[4]

Of course Sammler himself is hardly immune. He *explains* endlessly: to unruly students at Columbia, to make-shift "colleagues,"
to Govinda Lal, to impatient relatives and, most of all, to himself.
His anguish, like Herzog's, is that he cannot avoid the dreadful
implications of America's cultural moment. And rather than cash in
on *kitch*—by becoming a talk-show gladiator of the Mailer/Vidal
stripe—Bellow prefers to work off mounting irritations by having
Sammler say the following:

> Antiquity accepted models, the Middle Ages—I don't want to turn into
> a history book before your eyes—but modern man, perhaps because of
> collectivization, has a fever of originality. The idea of the uniqueness of
> the soul. An excellent idea. A true idea. But in these poor forms? Dear
> God! With hair, with clothes, with drugs, and cosmetics, with genitalia,
> with round trips through evil, monstrosity and orgy, with even God
> approached through obscenities? How terrified the soul must be in this
> vehemence, how little that is really dear to it it can see in these Sadic
> exercises. And even there, the Marquis de Sade in his crazy way was an
> Enlightenment philosopher. Mainly he intended blasphemy. But for
> those who follow (unaware) his recommended practises, the idea no
> longer is blasphemy, but rather hygiene, pleasure which is hygiene

too, and a charmed and *interesting* life. An *interesting* life is the supreme concept of dullards. (p. 229)

With *Mr. Sammler's Planet* (1970), action gives way to cultural meditation. But the progress suggests something about American letters as well. Writers like Hemingway or Faulkner had inspired nearly equal doses of homage and blasphemy, imitation and resistance, especially among practising novelists. It was hardly surprising when public honors like the Nobel Prize coincided with the moment their respective Modernisms threatened to lapse into self-parody. The Fifties, after all, were filled with Eisenhower, national apathy, the New Criticism, and, of course, J.D. Sallinger. Modernism hobbled along, but it had a self-conscious, academic ring. Sometime the mopping up operation took the form of literary criticism, pure and simple. On other occasions—say, in Bernard Malamud's *The Natural* (1952) or John Barth's *Giles Goat-Boy* (1966)—mythic structures were turned upside-down. Using Hemingway's sense of ritual (e.g. *The Sun Also Rises*) as a convenient benchmark, it looked as if contemporary writers had grabbed the wrong end of the stick. Now the stink of scholarship and the dust of library stacks replaced locker room odor and the weather-beaten trail.

Perhaps this accounts, at least in part, for the success of J.D. Salinger's *The Catcher in the Rye* (1951). Holden Caulfield was Huck Finn with a prep school tie, the protagonist of every authentically American saga. He is the eternal boy on the lam, holding off Corruption (which, in America, is synonymous with Adulthood) on one hand while he protects Innocence with the other. But he is also a fully realized fictional character, despite critical attempts to superimpose Vergil's *Aeneid* onto the nightmare of New York City. To be sure, Holden does battle with Death in ways that would tire even an epic Hero; from his nagging question about the fate of Central Park ducks to Phoebe's ominous "Daddy'll *kill* you!" Holden tries desperately to find the brakes on that infernal machine called mutability.

Unfortunately, in a world where the "phonies" are many and the "good guys" (Phoebe, the memory of his dead brother Allie, perhaps Mr. Antolini and, of course, Holden himself) are all too few, a nervous breakdown is never far away. Huck Finn lights out for the Western territories at the end of his archetypal journey; Holden unfolds his confessional monologue in a sanitarium, teetering somewhere between that madness we call clarity of vision and that confusion only an R. D. Laing could love.

Ironically enough, Holden's warning to chic performers like the Lunts or "old Ernie," the Village piano player, could apply with an equal force to Salinger himself: "If you do something *too* good, after a while, if you don't watch it, you start showing off. And then you're not good anymore." *The Catcher in the Rye* is a minor classic. Like the museum figures Holden meditates about, it will likely remain so. But the Glass family is another matter. Their neurotic disaffections parade through *Nine Stories* (1953), *Franny and Zooey* (1961) and *Seymour: An Introduction* (1963) until urban "cuteness" becomes a crushing bore. Another way of putting it might be this: *New Yorker* fiction of the Salinger mold tends, like a fine liqueur, to seem more rewarding in small doses. But given the loving attention heaped on, say, the Glass family medicine cabinet in *Franny and Zooey*, Salinger could not long avoid pejoratives like "precious," to say nothing of harsher judgments like "pretentious."

In large measure, the laurels which go with being the *New Yorker's* fair-haired boy passed to John Updike. If fantasized New Yorkers (who, once again, proved that Life has an itch to imitate Art—as *real* New Yorkers affected the postures of the already affected Glass clan) were Salinger's obsession, Updike has been hell-bent to bring high seriousness to the Protestant ethos. As a sheer *stylist*, of course, Updike remains a brilliant writer, but, for better or worse, Americans have always preferred a Theodore Dreiser to a Henry James. Still, novels like *Rabbit, Run* (1965) and its recent sequel—*Rabbit Redux* (1972)—are anchored squarely in that ordinary world a Salinger could never quite imagine.

But Salinger had all the elements necessary to ensure Success in the Fifties: characters formed from equal parts of sophistication and sensitivity, generous helpings of neuroses, a dash of *angst*, even some *ersatz* mysticism. Seymour Glass reigned as a virtually undisputed guru for an age which valued the tick of nonconformity hidden beneath its grey flannel suiting. After all, if *every* beleaguered high school student was Holden, every "sensitive" co-ed, Franny, it was fairly easy for graduates to rattle off the sort of book list a Salinger would approve. And if the acknowledged enemy was dullness, nervous breakdowns (especially if performed with *style*) were worth the risk. During those years navel-gazing became a popular indoor sport.

But the stifling stability of the Fifties (where the major problems seemed confined to Madison Avenue and suburbia) soon gave way to wide-ranging, but ill-defined, paranoia. [5] Someone—or, worse, SOMETHING—was controlling what the individual used to consider eminent domain. Joseph Heller called it *Catch 22* (1961) and the metaphor characterized much of the Sixties in the way that Eliot's waste land had for the Twenties. In such a world the comic and the terrible intertwine. The net effect travels under the convenient shorthand of Black Humor. It is as a loosely defined sensibility, then, that I will be discussing "black humor" and its radical dislocation of social norms and aesthetic traditions. Much the same situation applies to that slippery creature called the American-Jewish novel, although its history is longer and even more chequered. With writers like Kurt Vonnegut, Jr. and John Barth, I investigate the impulse toward "thin novels" in the former and highly reflexive ones in the latter. History-as-myth vs. myth-as-history is the center of my meditative chapter on the "new journalism" (Norman Mailer, Truman Capote, William Styron) and the problems of an ongoing fiction writer (Bernard Malamud). The study ends with a trio of fictionists—David Madden, Joyce Carol Oates and Isaac Bashevis Singer—who suggest that forward motion may be a matter of backward vision, that traditional techniques may be more rewarding than the promises of avant-garde experimentation.

What I have tried to imply with this zig-zagging account of the Post-Modernist's sense of backdrop and the special considerations he brings to his Art can, of course, be stated more simply: A critic chooses to talk about those writers who have moved him (either to anger or admiration) and *that*, more than any other factor, has been my rationale for the selections which follow. For my sins of omission, there will, I feel certain, be others who will want to give the Brautigans and Sukenicks their just deserts. At a certain point even a critic (non-heroic though he may be) must also say "The rest is silence." And as for my sins of commission, I take solace in the belief that fireworks begin when a book strikes against the critical grain, when somebody dares to suggest that our contemporary writers are parading themselves about without any clothes.

Notes

1   Leslie Fiedler, "Cross the Border, Close the Gap," *Playboy* (December 1969). Re-printed in *The Collected Essays of Leslie Fiedler*, II (New York: Stein and Day, 1971), 461. Subsequent references to Professor Fiedler are to this article.

2   In the *New Left,* Professor Kampf, at the time President of the Modern Language Association, summed up his feelings about culture and the Lincoln Center this way:

> Not a performance should go by without disruption. The fountains should be dried with calcium chloride, the statuary pissed on, the walls smeared with shit.

3   Saul Bellow, *Dangling Man* (New York: Vanguard Press, 1944), p. 9.

4   Saul Bellow, *Mr. Sammler's Planet* (New York: Viking, 1970), pp. 3-4. Subsequent references to *Mr. Sammler's Planet* are to this edition and pagination is given parenthetically.

5   In a world Post-Watergate, however, it is difficult—if not impossible—to talk about "paranoia." Perhaps a heightened sense of reality would be more like it.

II

The Graying of Black Humor

It was called *Black Humor* and, conveniently enough, Bantam published the paperback anthology in 1965, a point equidistant between the energy of beginnings and the exhaustion which would afflict it some five years later. Bruce Jay Friedman wrote the introductory remarks (his opening sentence: "I think I would have more luck defining an elbow or a corned-beef sandwich"[1] set the tone of artsy things to come) and authors like Joseph Heller, John Barth, Edward Albee, Vladimir Nabokow, J. P. Donleavy, and Terry Southern were included among the contributors.

One thing was clear: Black Humor was less a School than a Sensibility and more Protean than both. Their circle widened steadily, adding a Kurt Vonnegut here, a Thomas Berger there. The lens of Black Humor had a habit of stretching the world into grotesque shapes, of letting us in on the absurdity that was always there. No matter—scratch the surface of nearly any writer in the 1960's and there was sure to be a Black Humorist lurking around the edges somewhere.

All of which made precise definition not only difficult, but a little bit silly. Besides, nobody needed a literary barometer to tell them that Black Humor was in the air. The vital signs were obvious enough. And for those who continued to equate Black Humor with Dick Gregory or Godfrey Cambridge, nothing would help, not even a Bantam anthology. Therefore, what I propose to do is come at the theoretical aspects of Black Humor by way of those specifics which made for the rise-and-fall of Bruce Jay Friedman's fiction. Not because his achievements were more impressive than those of, say, Heller or Kesey or Barth, but, rather, because his novels represent Black Humor in its purest, which is to say, its most vulnerable state. And, too, it is a way of sneaking up on such triumphs of the 1960's as *Catch-22* or *One Flew Over The Cuckoo's Nest.*

We are hardly surprised when a contemporary novelist de-
clines rather than develops. By now the pattern of novel after
novel building on the substructure of an impressive, initial effort is
all too familiar. *Stern* (1962) is such a novel, the sort that is likely
to be resurrected when the furor about Black Humor is over and
Salinger no longer seems to be the alpha and omega of the Fifties.
It's all there in *Stern:* the uneasy Jewishness, the ulcers, the suburban situation. But the sense of terror about it all is actualized,
located in a compactness which never quite appears again in
Friedman's fiction.

Some fifteen years earlier Hollywood had imagined what the
complications of the pastoral homeowner might be like and called
it *Mr. Blandings Builds His Dream House.* Predictably enough, the
results were full of good cheer, even when nightmares gained on
dreams and Cary Grant seemed, almost, to lose his cool. *Stern*
shares much of the ambiance, but, this time, it is Kafka who looms
just beyond the klieg lights.

Stern is an angst-ridden apartment dweller, nose pressed
against suburbia while visions of extra rooms dance in his head:
"As a child he had graded the wealth of people by the number of
rooms in which they lived. He himself had been brought up in
three in the city and fancied people who lived in four were so much
more splendid than himself." [2]

But as Stern quickly discovers, he is not one of the Chosen
People who can make the exodus from the bondage of crowded
apartments to the Promised Land of suburban living. He is, at
best, a reluctant pioneer, a man who misses the cop on the beat,
the delicatessen at the corner.

And, too, the escalating costs—some real, some imagined—
have a way of upsetting the once eager homeowner:

> After moving in officially several days later, Stern hired a trio
> of Italian gardeners to prepare the elaborate shrubs for summer—two
> old, cackling, slow-moving ones and a fragrant and tempermental
> young man who spoke no English but had worked on the gardens of
> Italian nobility. The old men made straight borders along their flower
> beds, but the young man did his in curlicues, standing off after each
> twirl and making indications of roundness in the air with his hands.
> Their price was three dollars an hour, and as they moved along Stern

began to worry that they weren't working fast enough. He saw the shrub preparations costing him $800, leaving him no money for furniture. Stern wanted to tell the young man to stop doing the time-consuming curlicued borders and to do straight ones like the old men to keep the bill down. But he was afraid to say anything to a handsome young man who had worked on the grounds of Italian nobility. Stern watched the gardeners from inside the house, ducking behind a curtain so they wouldn't see him. He hoped they would hurry and perspired as the dollars ticked away in multiples of three. The old men rested on their rakes now, poking each other and cackling obscenely at the handsome young man as he made his temperamental curlicues. Then Stern lost sight of the young man and imagined that his long-nosed, great-eyed wife had inhaled his fragrance and dragged him with a sudden frenzy into the garage, her fingers digging through his black and oily young Italian hair, loving it so much more than Stern's thinning affair, which fell out now at the touch of a comb. (pp. 16-17)

Like the fantasized gardening bill, Stern's *tsoris* grows by multiples of three—anxieties float from his wallet to his hairline, only to rest (as they must) at the genitals. For Stern, cuckoldry—or the *threat* of cuckoldry—hides behind every suburban bush. But his schlemiel-hood has some distinctly modern wrinkles. Schlemiels of Yiddish humor were the architects of their own misfortune and the butts of condescending laughter. More often than not, the jokes told about them involved a cuckoldry which became even funnier when the victim staunchly denied it.

For example, in one classic story a man named Shemuliel returns home after a year of absence to find that his wife has given birth to a child. Although he may have had his doubts, the local rabbi established—by a long chain of pseudo-Talmudic reasoning—that the child was, indeed, his. Shemuliel had no choice; the verdict must be accepted. But his neighbors had no choice either. They laughed at such a character, if only to demonstrate that Shemuliel's fate was not theirs.

In another version of the same story, the setting is Chelem, a town famous for its comic "wise men":

A young scholar of Chelem, innocent in the ways of earthly matters, was stunned one morning when his wife gave birth. Pellmell he ran to the rabbi.

' Rabbi,' he blurted out, 'an extraordinary thing has happened!

Please explain it to me. My wife has just given birth although we have
been married only three months! How is this possible? Everyone knows
that it takes nine months for a baby to be born!'

'My son,' he said. 'I can see you haven't the slightest idea about
such matters, nor can you make the simplest calculation. Let me ask
you: Have you lived with your wife three months?'

'Yes.'

'She has lived with you three months?'

'Yes.'

'Together—have you lived three months?'

'Yes.'

'What's the total then—three months plus three months plus
three?'

'Nine months, Rabbi!'

'*Nu.* . . so what is the problem?'[3]

Isaac Bashevis Singer's "Gimpel the Fool" is cut from a similar bolt
of cloth, although, this time, the roles are reversed. Gimpel is more
saint than schlemiel; the deceptions of this world become less important than the realities of the next.

In Stern's case the schlemielhood is internalized, more a
matter of fantasy than fact. The dreaded "kike man"—who insulted
his child, pushed his wife and, possibly, caught a glimpse of her
crotch—becomes the beast of his suburban jungle, the figure in his
psychotic carpet. All the elements of Stern's deepest fears—his
ambivalences about Judaism, Gentiles and sexuality—are neatly
combined in his anti-Semitic neighbor. Suddenly Stern's floating
anxieties have found an anchor, a physical embodiment for all the
undefinable terrors.

But beseiged by problems on all sides—caterpillars devour his
garden; dogs attack him on a nightly basis—Stern prefers to sub-
stitute an evergrowing number of self-generated (and, thereby,
controllable) fears for the one who lives just down the street. He

pictures the police as "large, neutral-faced men with rimless glasses who would accuse him of being a newcomer making vague trouble-making charges." Especially if he complains about the threatening dogs. "They would take him into a room and hit him in his large, white, soft stomach." And so he swallows his impulse, only to then imagine himself "fighting silently in the night with the two gray dogs, lasting eight minutes and then being found a week later with open throat by small Negro children."

Some of the best sections in *Stern* are flashbacks, designed to deal with the problem of being called a "kike." In J. D. Salinger's "Down by the Dinghy," Boo Boo Glass defuses the ugly epithet by skillfully changing it to "kite," something her assimilated son can understand. But Stern knows all too well that the word is *supposed* to hurt. And, yet, it is hard for him to make a viable connection between a Judaic tradition and his individual experiences. The vignettes which result are filled with poignant alienation. And in the best of them Friedman is able to strike a balance between the humor and the pathos of his material:

> As a boy, Stern had been taken to holiday services, where he stood in ignorance among bowing, groaning men who wore brilliantly embroidered shawls. Stern would do some bows and occasionally let fly a complicated imitative groan, but when he sounded out he was certain one of the old genuine groaners had spotted him and knew he was issuing a phony. Stern thought it was marvelous that the old men knew exactly when to bow and knew the groans and chants and melodies by heart. He wondered if he would ever get to be one of their number. He went to Hebrew school, but there seemed to be no time at all devoted to theatrical bows and groans, and even with three years of Hebrew school under his belt Stern still felt a loner among the chanting sufferers at synagogues. After a while he began to think you could never get to be one of the groaners through mere attendance at Hebrew school. You probably had to pick it all up in Europe. (p. 43)

But, alas, Black Humor is often a study in excess and Friedman has a nasty habit of overplaying his cards. Stern's father, for example, contributed puns on "orange Jews" or "prune Jews," while his college roommates coin the term "Gee-yoo." None of this low-brow banter has much to do with Stern, to say nothing of his long-postponed confrontation with the "kike man."

In fact, the "kike man"—Stern discovers he is named De

Luccio—remains more a fixation than a developed character, the focus of Stern's ever-widening projections:

> Stern took note of every detail of the man's house, a new one registering each night as he drove by. A television aerial. This was good. It meant the communications industry was getting through to the man, subtly driving home messages of Brotherhood. But he imagined the man watching only Westerns, contemptuously flicking off all shows that spoke of tolerance. Stern saw himself writing and producing a show about fair play, getting it shown one night on every channel, and forcing the man to watch it since the networks would be bare of Westerns. (p. 41)

With all this we are scarcely surprised when Stern's x-rays unearth a duodenal ulcer. After all, he is riddled by equal doses of repression and anxiety—and to clinch the cliché, he works for a Madison Avenue ad agency! Of course Stern's ulcer is the "kike man" internalized, but somehow, knowing that doesn't help. The same is true of Stern's breakdown. It may be physically inevitable, but that hardly makes it aesthetically earned. In fact, only his periodic fantasies about cuckoldry manage to keep the threat of Friedman's novel alive. For example, when his wife drives him to the asylum,

> . . . Stern watched his wife's (feet), apart as they worked the pedals; he imagined her dropping him off at the home, then going immediately to a service station and allowing the attendant to make love to her while her feet kept working the pedals so that she could always say that she had driven all the way home without stopping. (pp. 92-93)

More and more of the novel is consumed by built-in victories of this stripe. As Stern's *extension ad absurdem* argument would have it, De Luccio stands—symbolically if you will—for all that he despises: De Luccio's veteran's jacket dredges up visions of militaristic might, while his softball playing, beer-drinking style of Gentile life is hostile to all the vague Judaic traditions Stern holds dear.

In a telling review of J. P. Donleavy's recent novel, *The Onion Eaters*, Anatole Broyard catalogues the desperate lengths some critics will go to avoid announcing the book in question is just plain bad:

> If a book is painfully bad, it can always be praised in words beginning
> with "r," such as ribald, rollicking, ravaging or riveting. In desperate
> cases, reviewers can fall back on zany, irreverent or outrageous. When
> a book seems to make no sense at all, to offer nothing recognizable to
> the reader, it is sure to be described as bursting the confines of the
> conventional novel.[4]

All of Broyard's epithets could apply to the asylum sections of
Stern. But the nub of the problem is as old as Aristotle, as old-
fashioned as terms like plot or dramatic unity. Ending a novel has
become increasingly difficult for the modern writer. Kafka comes
to mind immediately, but his is not an isolated case. For the Black
Humorist, however, the problem takes on some interesting twists.
His is a fiction of comic fantasies, of "bits" which owe a greater
debt to the stand-up comedian than the sit-down novelist. They
depend upon rapid-fire delivery and comic pacing, but not the
comprehensive vision or actualized characterization we associate
with the novel.

In *Stern,* Friedman concentrated on such middle-aged phenomena as cuckoldry and the problems of Gentile suburbia. In *A
Mother's Kisses* (1964), the psychodynamics of Black Humor
shrink to Momism and the difficulties of getting into college. But,
more importantly, the aesthetics of Black Humor give *A Mother's
Kisses* that same touch of the grotesque Milo Minderbinder brings
to the art of war profiteering. Excess is the heart of the matter.
Realistic elements are stretched until the resulting fabric has that
curiously elongated look we associate with fun house mirrors.
Unfortunately, a great many contemporary writers who enjoy being
"lost in the funhouse" lack John Barth's verbal talent for getting
out. All too often the technique degenerates into a mere gimmick,
a blank check issued to the unbridled imagination. For example,
Sophie Portnoy—that comic villainess of Philip Roth's *Portnoy's
Complaint*—may be the apotheosis of the Jewish mother, but
Friedman's is only a push or two away. Portnoy's mother *kvetches*;
Joseph's mother drools. No matter, a paperback Freud covers them
both. And when you add a pre-Consciousness III hysteria about
college acceptance, the results are likely to go something like this:

> He [i.e. Joseph] saw himself letting a year go by, then reapplying
> only to find himself regarded as a suspicious leftover fellow, his appli-
> cation tossed onto a pile labeled 'repeaters,' not to be read until all

the fresh new ones had been gone through. Year after year would slip away, until finally, at thirty-seven, he would enter night school along with a squad of newly naturalized Czechs, sponsored by labor unions and needing a great many remedial reading sessions.   .   .   .

> His mother seemed to put colleges in the same category as sold-out musicals and jammed restaurants.   .   .   . Once, a special kitchen-type chair had been set up for him in the aisle of a hit revue; he had watched the show tensely, expecting at any second to be tapped on the shoulder by higher authorities and told to take his chair out of the aisle.   .   .   . Now he had a vision of her dragging him through lines of students to the bursar at nostalgic old Wesleyan or tradition-haunted V.M.I., asking him if he could 'do a little something for the kid.' And Joseph pictured himself in freshman classes, sitting in a special kitchen chair off to the side of professorial daises. [5]

The literature of the sixties is filled with whiners, some serious (and likely to be found in novels by Saul Bellow), others comfortably comic. Joseph belongs to the latter group. His fantasies are a strategy of control rather than a means of confrontation. And herein lies the difference between the darkly comic visions of, say, a Melville or Faulkner and the pale copy that is *A Mother's Kisses.* It has become fashionable to blame the whole thing on affluence, as if the shoddy culture of the last twenty years made genuinely serious Art impossible. But the *real* issue I suspect is courage. *A Mother's Kisses* remains a superficial novel because it steadfastly refuses to face its own implications or to deal honestly with the enigmatic. Friedman relies, instead, on systematic evasions, preferring a fantasy of his own comic making to the existential stuff of fiction already there.

To be sure, the Black Humorist has been twice-scooped: first, by those Modernist giants who gave the inner life that thick, fictional proof it demanded and then by the quality of contemporary life itself. As Friedman himself put it:

> What has happened is that the satirist has had ground usurped by the newspaper reporter. The journalist, who in the year 1964, must cover the ecumenical debate on whether Jews, on the one hand, are still to be known as Christ-killers or, on the other hand are to be let off the hook, is certainly today's satirist. The novelist-satirist, with no real territory of his own to roam, has had to discover new land, invent a new currency, a new set of filters, has had to sail into darker waters somewhere out beyond satire and I think this is what is meant by

black humor.[6]

And, yet, behind all the brave rhetoric—like Tennyson's "Ulysses," Black Humor will "strive, to seek, to find, and not to yield"—lies the sort of whine I have been talking about. Genuine satire is tougher-minded and tighter-lipped. It takes a hard look at the absurdities of life and an even harder one at human illusions. Friedman, however, would have us believe that the only alternative for the contemporary satirist lies in outdoing the headlines, no matter what the aesthetic cost. The result is a curious sort of escalation; life forces the would-be writer from the outrageous to the zany and, ultimately, exhausts him in the process. The mechanics of Black Humor become all too predictable, in fact, tedious. And, ironically enough, we quickly learn how to be comfortable with the most grotesque and/or irreverant news such an aesthetic has to offer.

Joseph's mother begins as a vulgar cliché; Friedman's touch merely raises it to the second power. For example, she follows her son to summer camp one day—rather like Mary's little lamb, but with more staying power—and then the next, setting up a base of sexual activity just across the lake. When Joseph is finally accepted to Kansas Land Grant Agricultural (where courses like "the history and principles of agriculture" and "feed chemistry" comprise the curriculum) Mom insists on coming too. Add a handful of zany minor characters and the drift toward self-parody is complete.

Still, there are moments in *A Mother's Kisses* when the terrors of contemporary life are rendered with sharp, even metaphorical, precision:

> A long line had formed in the men's room, leading to a single urinal, which was perched atop a dais. When a fellow took too long, there were hoots and catcalls such as 'What's the matter, fella, can't you find it?' As his turn came nearer, Joseph began to get nervous. He stepped before the urinal finally, feeling as though he had marched out onto a stage. He stood there a few seconds, then zipped himself up and walked off. The man in back of him caught his arm in a vise and said, 'You didn't go. I watched.' (p. 184)

Very little of Kafka's flavor is lost in the translation. And the hand which descends to unmask our smallest deception strikes us as real, all too real.

In *A Mother's Kisses* Black Humor meets the Oedipus complex, but the results are hardly decisive. Friedman's irreverence is matched by his self-consciousness and the long shadows of puerile comedy fall everywhere. With his latest novel, *The Dick* (1970), the focus centers on the world of law-and-order. Friedman means to draw a parallel between sexuality and crime fighting, as the title of the novel and the name of its protagonist, LePeters, suggests. Nor do the bad jokes stop there. When LePeters has his psychological interview, the conversation goes something like this:

> 'What do you think all these guns around here represent?' he asked LePeters in a lightening change of subject.

> 'Oh, I don't know,' said LePeters. 'Phalluses, I guess.' Actually, he had dipped into a textbook or two and was taking a not-so-wild shot.

> 'Not bad,' said Worthway, lifting one crafty finger in the Heidelberg style and making ready to leave. 'But some of them are pussies, too.'[7]

Outraging the already outrageous is a full-time, desperate, activity in *The Dick*. And, yet, there are spots here too when Friedman's satire is right on target:

> 'You know who I hate,' said the cop. 'I don't hate Eichmann. Oh no, not really. And I don't hate Hitler either. Not down deep. You know who I hate?'

> 'Who's that?'

> 'Anyone who does crime in the street.' (p. 51)

But, alas, such sharpness is rare. Generally, the pitch in *The Dick* is shrill, filled with excess and buffoonery. Friedman's description of LePeters (clippings expert and homicide department PR man) is a good example:

> On his desk was an empty silver holster in which he kept his pencils and glue brush; pinned to his large chest was a 'baby badge,' an exact replica of the real thing, although scaled down to half the standard size. . . . He took great pride in his clipping displays, always making sure to give them some slant or focus so that homicide chiefs, at a single glance, might get the drift of the week's slaughter. In this partic-

ular layout, he had placed the suicide of a video kingpin in the center of the page and then bordered it with what he considered an ironic, point-making fringe of vicious little fruit-stabbings. (p. 4)

LePeters is a study in ballooning ambivalence. His face is divided by a childhood scar, one side suggesting the Jewishness of his Sussman past, while the other speaks to his LePeters' present. He vacillates between the sentiments of a liberal and those of a dick. Part of him had "read Moby Dick in one sitting. . . . Hadn't he thought of death and infinity, wrestling with the precise structure of time until his teeth ached and his eyeballs, like tiny runaway planets, did backward loops in his head." Surely *that* is not the sensibility of a dick! And, yet, LePeters/Sussman is plagued by another part of his nature, one which suggests empathy (rather than revulsion) with everything dickdom stands for:

> Could he actually say that his heart was quiet when he heard 'The Star Spangled Banner' or saw the Marines storm a beachhead on a late-night Iwo Jima movie? When some dick proposed that we settle our differences with the Red world by 'lobbing a few into the Kremlin men's room,' wasn't there one slender pocket within him in which for a frozen instant the question was asked, 'Why not?' LePeters had cop in him all right, more than he liked to admit. . . . His heart went out to black people, killers and saints alike, but what about that fractional component in him that got a brief shiver of pleasure when a barefoot, defenseless Negro got smashed in the head until he confessed a phantom crime. (pp. 284-285)

The result is a comic war, one LePeters wages with decidedly mixed feelings. *The Dick* is full of traditional themes—paranoia, cuckoldry and diluted Jewishness—but Friedman fails to raise such normally congenial material to anything above a sophomoric snicker.

Friedman's declining canon demonstrates that Black Humor alone makes for a limited—and often shaky—foundation on which to build a novel. To be sure, the graying of Black Humor afflicted others as well. A graph of, say, Thomas Pynchon's spectacular rise-and-fall would look much the same, although *Gravity's Rainbow* (1973) takes considerable steam out of my generalization. His first book, *V* (1963), was thick and probably overpraised. Like the ubiquitous V, Joyce's footprints were everywhere—and that influence is even more strongly felt in Pynchon's latest "epic." But for all the good cheer of metaphorical yo-yo's, alligator hunts in the New York sewer system, Esther's hilarious nose job or the schlemielhood of Benny Profane, the net result evaporates. On the other hand, Pynchon's next effort—a paranoid romp through Southern California called *The Crying of Lot 49* (1966)—was frustrating, plain hard-to-read. People got caught—rather than "caught up"—in the traps and implications of a protagonist called Oedipa Maas. *Gravity's Rainbow* recouped whatever losses Pynchon may have suffered and, once again, Black Humor and world-wide paranoia promise to keep the literary de-coders very, very busy.

Which brings me to Joseph Heller's *Catch-22* (1961) and Ken Kesey's *One Flew Over The Cuckoo's Nest* (1963). In these novels Black Humor shades into the larger concerns of an Absurdist vision and the stakes are raised all around. This is not to suggest that other practitioners in the art of Black Humor lacked a sense of the Absurd, but, rather, that Heller and Kesey took it more seriously. Generally speaking Black Humor tends to pick on easy targets— Mom, apple pie, flags and all the rest. With Heller and Kesey, however, death crawls into the mask of comedy and, suddenly, *"gallenhumor"* is only a short step from the gallows itself. In *Catch-22*, for example, the comic and the terrible intertwine with disturbing regularity:

> The soldier in white was encased from head to toe in plaster and gauze. He had two useless legs and two useless arms. . . . Sewn into the bandages over the insides of both elbows were zippered lips through which he was fed clear fluid from a clear jar. A silent zinc pipe rose from the cement on his groin and was coupled to a slim rubber hose that carried waste from his kidneys and dropped it efficiently into a clear, stoppered jar on the floor. When the jar on the floor was full, the jar feeding his elbow was empty, and the two were simply switched quickly so that stuff could drip back into him.8

The result is a darkly comic Sisyphus, one even Camus might have trouble justifying in Existentialist terms. But, more importantly, the passage suggests a synecdoche of the novel itself. The structure of *Catch-22* is fluid, forever circling back upon itself in an attempt to understand that figure in the cockpit who is Snowden. On the other hand, the bombing missions grow in a relentlessly linear— which is to say, "logical"—fashion. The zig-zagging chronology— filled with flashbacks and/or deliberate interruptions—is Yossarian's way of bringing forward motion to a halt.

And, too, it provides that bare margin of safety necessary for comic relief. The absurdities remain, but Yossarian manages to generate a certain amount of good cheer as each new one is discovered and carefully catalogued:

> All the officer patients of the ward were forced to censor letters written by all the enlisted-men patients. . . . To break the monotony he [i.e. Yossarian] invented games. Death to all modifiers, he declared one day, and out of every letter that passed through his hands went every adverb and every adjective. The next day he made war on articles. He reached a much higher plane of creativity the following day when he blacked out everything in the letters but *a, an* and *the*. That erected more dynamic intralinear tensions, he felt, and in just about every case left a message far more universal. (p. 8)

Minor characters abound, although all of them seem to be cut from the same bolt of inverted expectations which produced a Colonel Cargill:

> Colonel Cargill, General Peckem's troubleshooter, was a forceful, ruddy man. Before the war he had been an alert, very bad marketing executive. Colonel Cargill was so awful a marketing executive that his services were much sought after by firms eager to establish losses for tax purposes. Throughout the civilized world, from Battery Park to Fulton Street, he was known as a dependable man for a fast tax write-off. His prices were high, but failure did not come easily. He had to start at the top and work his way down, and with sympathetic friends in Washington, losing money was no simple matter. It took months of hard work and careful misplanning. A person misplaced, disorganized, miscalculated, overlooked everything and opened every loophole, and just when he thought he had it made, the government gave him a lake or a forest or an oilfield and spoiled everything. Even with such handicaps, Colonel Cargill could be relied on to run the most prosperous enterprise into the ground. He was a self-made man and he owed his lack of success to nobody. (p. 28)

The humor in *Catch-22* is laid on thick, perhaps *too* thick. Repetition has a way of dulling the appetite, especially when the teams were divided into good guys vs. bad guys so early in the game. Ultimately, though, Yossarian learns Snowden's grisly secret: "Man was matter. . . . Drop him out a window and he'll fall. Set fire to him and he'll burn. Bury him and he'll rot like other kinds of garbage." And *that*, rather than "catch-22," is the heart of the novel. The pragmatic Orr understood it early—and such is the stuff of which survival is made:

> Each time he [i.e. Yossarian] caught himself worrying he made himself remember that Orr could do everything and broke into silent laughter at the picture of Orr in the raft as Sergeant Knight had described him, bent forward with a busy, preoccupied smile over the map and compass in his lap, stuffing one soaking-wet chocolate bar after another into his grinning, tittering mouth as he paddled away dutifully through the lightning, thunder and rain with the bright blue useless toy oar, the fishing line with dried bait trailing out behind him. (p. 326)

As the pun on his name suggests, Orr is the alternative to Yossarian's brand of comic rebellion. But it is a strange note on which to end the novel. Suddenly all bets are off, including the mushrooming empire of Milo Minderbinder, the infinite power of ex-PFC Wintergreen and the force of "catch-22" itself. Yossarian drops the capital-I Innocence which has been his trademark for some 450 pages and bolts for Sweden. Like the "soldier in white," perhaps Heller thought it was time to reverse the jars.

But if *Catch-22* provided a convenient metaphor of the bureaucratic double-shuffle—one which could be applied, with equal force, to insurance companies and college presidents—Ken Kesey's *One Flew Over The Cuckoo's Nest* provided its manual of arms. All the allegorical elements were there: the Combine, Big Nurse and, of course, Randall Patrick McMurphy. As Chief Bromden puts it, the asylum is "Like a cartoon world, where the figures are flat and outlined in black, jerking through some kind of goofy story that might be real funny if it weren't for the cartoon figures being real guys."[9]

However, it *is* laughter—albeit of a very special sort—which is at the heart of McMurphy's self-styled rebellion. And his arguments go something like this:

> You know, that's the first thing that got me about this place, that there wasn't anybody laughing. I haven't heard a real laugh since I came through that door, do you know that? Man, when you lose your laugh you lose your *footing*. A man go around lettin' a woman whup him down till he can't laugh any more, and he loses one of the biggest edges he's got on his side. (pp. 65-66)

The speech reads like an echo of Stubb's philosophy in Melville's dark epic *Moby-Dick*:

> Ha! ha! ha! ha! hem! clear my throat!—I've been thinking over

> it ever since, and that ha ha's the final consequence. Why so? Because
> a laugh's the wisest, easiest answer to all that's queer: and come what
> will, one comfort's always left. . . . I know not all that may be
> coming, but be it what it will, I'll go to it laughing.

The identification is somewhat strengthened by the whales which
decorate McMurphy's shorts and the oblique allusions he makes
concerning them: " 'From a co-ed at Oregon State, Chief, a Literary
major.' He snaps the elastic with his thumb. 'She gave them to me
because she said I was a symbol.' " However, for a writer who draws
so heavily on conventional devices—a mental institution in which
the patients should, presumably, be freed and their keepers committed; an All-American Bitch (complete with oversized breasts); a
predictably impotent psychiatrist, etc.—such gingerly attitudes
about literary symbolism hardly seem appropriate.

Moreover, there are scenes when the Black Humor of
Cuckoo's Nest inverts a cliché with the best of them. For example:

> One Christmas at midnight on the button, at the old place, the
> ward door blows open with a crash, and in comes a fat man with a
> beard, eyes ringed red by the cold and his nose just the color of a
> cherry. The black boys get him cornered in the hall with flashlights.
> I see he's all tangled in the tinsel Public Relations has been stringing
> all over the place, and he's stumbling around in it in the dark. He's
> shading his red eyes from the flashlights and sucking on his mustache.
>
> 'Ho ho ho,' he says. 'I'd like to stay but I must be hurrying along.
> Very tight schedule, ya know. Ho ho. Must be going. . .'
>
> The black boys move in with flashlights. They kept him with us
> six years before they discharged him, clean-shaven and skinny as a
> pole. (p. 70)

On the other hand, McMurphy's humor is a survival technique, one that is as potent as Yossarian's was ineffectual:

> 'Mr. Bibbit, you might warn this Mr. Harding that I'm so crazy
> that I admit voting for Eisenhower.'
>
> 'Bibbit! You tell Mr. McMurphy I'm so crazy I voted for
> Eisenhower twice!'
>
> 'And you tell Mr. Harding right back'—he puts both hands on

the table and leans down, his voice getting low—'that I'm so crazy I plan to vote for Eisenhower again this *November*.' (p. 24)

The memory of a freezing Snowden haunts Yossarian. In *Cuckoo's Nest*, Ellis performs a similar, though less obvious, function for McMurphy. At first glance, however, his future as a literary device looks doubtful:

> He's there pulling Ellis's hand off the wall and shaking it just like he was a politician running for something and Ellis's vote was good as anybody's. 'Buddy,' he says to Ellis in a solemn voice, 'my name is R. P. McMurphy and I don't like to see a fullgrown sloshin' around in his own water. Whyn't you go get dried up?'
>
> Ellis looks down at the puddle around his feet in pure surprise. 'Why, I thank you,' he says and even moves off a few steps toward the latrine, before the nails pull his hands back to the wall. (p. 25)

Later, when the Acutes leaves for a fishing expedition, "Ellis pulled his hands down off the nails in the wall and squeezed Billy Bibbit's hand and told him to be a fisher of men." Then, according to Bromden, "McMurphy led the twelve of us to the sea."

For all the Black Humor about Christ patterns, the novel itself moves toward self-sacrifice and redemption—with McMurphy as the reluctant Lamb:

> Why should it be me goes to bat at these meetings over these piddling little gripes about keeping the dorm door open and about cigarettes in the Nurses' Station? I couldn't figure it at first, why you guys were coming to me like I was some kind of savior. Then I just happened to find out about the way the nurses have the big say as to who gets discharged and who doesn't. And I got wise awful damned fast. I said, 'Why those slippery bastards have *conned* me, snowed me into holding their bag. If that don't beat all, conned ol' R. P. McMurphy. '(p.166)

And so they had. But, in a larger sense, McMurphy had conned himself and the cost of that commitment—rather than the paranoia about Combines—is what makes *Cuckoo's Nest* a significant novel. After all, the allegorical trappings of the book—Big Nurse, the Combine, etc.—are both constant and all too predictable. Only McMurphy changes. And *his* growth—from con-man to dying god— makes a change in others possible.

In the final analysis, Black Humor provided an angle of vision for some, a comic technique for others. It is understandable enough that they were spoken of a seamless unit, but Bruce Jay Friedman is dead right when he describes his fellow Black Humorists as "separate writers who could not care less about one another and are certainly not going to attend any bi-monthly meetings to discuss policy and blackball new members." Of course things looked brighter for the Black Humorist in 1965. Since then Heller's regular promises to finish his second novel (with *Something Happened* [1975] he finally has!) are only matched by Administration spokesmen who see light at the end of dark, Vietnamese tunnels. Kesey, of course, has abandoned fiction altogether. And those clouds which do remain have begun to look gray—very gray indeed.

Notes

1   Bruce Jay Friedman, ed., *Black Humor* (New York: Bantam, 1965), vii.

2   Bruce Jay Friedman, *Stern* (New York: Simon and Schuster, 1963), p. 12
     Subsequent references to *Stern* are to this edition and pagination is given
     parenthetically.

3   Sanford Pinsker, *The Schlemiel as Metaphor* (Carbondale: Southern
     Illinois University Press, 1971), pp. 15-16.

4   Anatole Broyard, "The Irrevocable Reputation," New York Times
     (July 15, 1971), 33.

5   Bruce Jay Friedman, *A Mother's Kisses* (New York: Simon and Schuster,
     1964), p. 57. Subsequent references to *A Mother's Kisses* are to this
     edition and pagination is given parenthetically.

6   *Black Humor*, p. x.

7   Bruce Jay Friedman, *The Dick* (New York: Alfred A. Knopf, 1970), p. 15.
     Subsequent references to *The Dick* are to this edition and pagination is
     given parenthetically.

8   Joseph Heller, *Catch-22* (New York: Dell edition, 1974), p. 10. Subse-
     quent references to *Catch-22* are to this edition and pagination is given
     parenthetically.

9   Ken Kesey, *One Flew Over the Cuckoo's Nest* (New York: Viking Press,
     1963), p. 34. Subsequent references to *One Flew Over the Cuckoo's Nest*
     are to this edition and pagination is given parenthetically.

III

The Rise-and-Fall of the American-Jewish Novel

"American-Jewish" has always been a clumsy term, one that makes for confusions all around. And this is particularly true where the literary enterprise is concerned. But the hyphen has been the villain for too long now; it merely tries to bind alternating currents with the shorthand of convenience. The deeper problem has to do with the nature of what has come to be called "Jewish writing" *per se*. Actually, it makes more sense to talk about literature in Hebrew or Yiddish or whatever, identifying the writing by that language in which it was written. Strictly speaking, there *is* no "Jewish" literature. Rather, the "Jewishness" is a matter of content: a commentary on the Talmud or homiletics about *Tanakh* would qualify, but not the "stories" of people like Bernard Malamud or Saul Bellow or even Isaac Bashevis Singer. Theirs is a writing which tends to distract—rather than enhance—the study of sacred texts. And to the devoutly religious, this is called *bittel Torah*, a waste of time.

Time is really the heart of the matter, especially as it takes the form of a confrontation between the forces of the sacred and those of the profane. God's words—as revealed on Sinai—are eternal; man's are not. Therefore, that painful moment when the religious temper and the creative drive must part company becomes, in a word, inevitable.

But for a person both "Jewish" *and* would-be writer, the choice has a nasty habit of being indefinitely postponed. The umbrella of institutional Judaism simply widens to accommodate— and, hopefully, de-fuse—its potential troublemakers. A clean break is virtually impossible. The conflict is a longstanding one, although we tend to see its outlines most vividly in the explosions of secular energy which characterized ghetto life during the latter years of the nineteenth century. The homogeneous and highly regulated life of Orthodox Judaism gave way gradually to a welters of "isms":

political Zionism, Socialism, trade unionism. Free-thinkers challenged the rabbis, Orthodox fathers mourned for secular sons, but the outside world had made the handwriting on the ghetto walls quite clear: the old God of Sinai was dead. Long live Darwin or Freud or Marx or whatever the newer gods might call themselves.

Of course the transition was neither as smooth nor as instantaneous as my thumbnail sketch implies. Rabbinic authority may have declined, but the Traditions they represented were still viable, at least as far as providing common denominators of language and mythic structure were concerned. For the secularists, it was the stuff of which substructures could be made. And, too, it was on just such foundations that they forged their separate, and often contradictory, visions of the good life. It is hardly surprising that, once again, the "Jewish" writer found himself caught in the squeeze. The rabbis had demanded allegiance to a concept of *Takhlis* or "purpose" commensurate with Orthodox life; the secularists simply extended the notion to include amendments of their own. Now they demanded that "stories" glorify the worker, help the garment union. To the old yardstick of *takhlis* new requirements had been added. The more things changed, the more they stayed the same.

The result was in-fighting of the purest sort. Verbal warfare broke out everywhere: in endless pamphlets, in street-corner rhetoric, in tightly drawn ideological lines. Some of the spirit which Cynthia Ozick captures in her brilliant novella, *Envy, Or Yiddish In America* manages to survive, but the passion which pitted Yiddish against Hebrew or English against them both has all but disappeared.

In the comfort of retrospect such wars cannot help looking a bit silly. No propaganda, however impassioned the cause or flashy the polemical argument, is a match for history itself. Moreover, history has a cunning of its own. What I have called a Judaic substructure—that is, those intertwining strands of religion and culture—provided the necessary springboard from which secularist proposals were launched. Ironically enough, what the early secularists could assume as a fund of Jewish common knowledge could not be sustained, even if co-existence had been the rule rather than the exception. And as this supporting fabric systematically eroded, the superstructure of secularist culture was cut off from those very materials which had made for both cohesion and resistance. There was no need to make an official announcement or set an exact date for the phenomenon. When a tradition is sophisticated enough to become self-conscious, the evidence that its vitality has been lost is already there. The most interesting American-Jewish novels either foreshadow this condition—as is the case with Abraham Cahan's *The Rise Of David Levinsky* in 1917—or, like Henry Roth's *Call It Sleep* (1934), manage to give the contradictory impulses toward assimilation their fullest expression.

Such tensions may be the raw materials of Art, but the insular world of the lower East Side made the resulting novels seem embarrassingly parochial. After all, the literary mainstream had moved elsewhere—to Paris or Pamplona or an imaginatively reconstructed Dublin—and, for better or worse, it was Joyce's Bloom and Hemingway's Cohn who dominated the Gentile imagination. The ironies that resulted were bitter ones, particularly when all the missed directions and crossed purposes took shape. For example, a figure like the "wandering Jew" evoked radically different responses depending upon "when" and "to where" you crossed the Atlantic. For the disillusioned expatriate, it was an apt metaphor of the Modernist condition. And whether the treatment was by Joyce (Bloom as literature's quintessential wanderer) or Hemingway (Cohn as capital-A Alien among the already alienated), Gentile writers plumbed the Jewish psyche and its fascinating "difference" at the very moment when most American—Jewish writers were seeking a kind of salvation in assimilated sameness. Besides, expatriation had small appeal for a people who had been in various stages of expatriation since 70 C. E. Like Huck Finn, they had been there—and, in the 1920's, they were happy enough to "stay home" in that "Golden Land" they called America.

All this made for a radical Americanization. Yiddish newspapers armed the immigrant with pragmatic advice about everything from politics to table etiquette, shamelessly designed to make the transition from "greenhorn" to "American" as speedy as possible. Yiddish may have been the medium of the marketplace, the language of *dos folk*, but it was the Educational Alliance Building—and its night school classes in English—which represented their collective aspirations. Even Abraham Cahan, editor of the highly influential *Forward* and a novelist in his own right, would have agreed. For him, a Yiddish newspaper was a sometime thing, one that, to use a Marxist metaphor, would shrivel away when the job of assimilation was completed.

By now the scenerio is all too familiar. Up-from-the-ghetto sagas may differ in degree (depending upon the mix of hostility and/or nostalgia they contain) but such novels are depressingly alike in kind. In Norman Podhoretz's *Making It*, however, the "brutal contract"—that tacit agreement between a majority (read: WASP) culture and an aspiring minority—was writ in large letters. Podhoretz's success story includes all the standard elements: poverty in Brooklyn, affluence at *Commentary* and the appropriate stops at the appropriate educational watering holes in between. But *Making It* is out for bigger game than its structure could provide. The good news Podhoretz comes to bear is this: *success* has become the "dirty little secret" of our society in much the way that sex was for D. H. Lawrence's. One can discuss a current affair over cocktails, but not a recent promotion. So much for the limits of contemporary "liberation." And as Podhoretz himself suspected, reviewers found more of the "tasteless" than the brilliant in this self-styled sociology of success.

And yet, the notion of a brutal contract is a useful wedge into those knotty problems which faced the Jewish writer in America. The vaudeville stage, for example, was filled with an array of un-American stereotypes—the shuffling, banjo-eyed Negro, the drunken Irishman and the money-hungry Jew—all designed to speed up assimilation at the expense of ethnic characteristics. Soon the brutal contract was fulfilled. The substructure which a previous generation had rejected could, now, be safely ignored.

All this put the would-be writer in a curious position. He had majored in English literature and, more often than not, had earned Honors in Anglophilism, familiar with Donne but not Dubnow; able to draw elaborate charts of Milton's cosmology, but unsure of the distinction between *mishnah* and *gemarrah*, the American-Jewish writer was far more "American" than he was "Jewish." Some years ago Leslie Fiedler half-jokingly suggested the following model of his progress:

> It might be possible, indeed, to make a graph showing, decade by decade, the point at which it became possible for Jews:

(1) to act out travesties of themselves on the stage;

(2) to act out travesties of other "comical" ethnic groups (Chico Marx as an Italian, Al Jolson in blackface);

(3) to write popular songs and patriotic sub-poetry and begin the wholesale entry into universities as students;

(4) to produce comic strips and popular novels;

(5) to argue cases in court and judge them from the bench, to prescribe for the common cold and analyze the neurotic;

(6) to write prose fiction and anti-academic criticism;

(7) to teach in the universities and help determine official taste in the arts;

(8) to write serious poetry, refuse to go to college, and write on the walls, 'Down with the Jews!' [1] (pp. 67-68)

To such a list one might add the following: to offer courses in the American-Jewish novel and to teach them to students who "research" what their grandparents had struggled hard to "forget."

In short, the *center* could not long hold, particularly without that fragile combination of a cohesive locale (i.e. the lower East Side) and an Operative Tradition. The energy which made for in-fighting as well as accomplishment had been dissipated—and what Leslie Fiedler has called the "Judiazation of America" (Huck Finn becoming Augie March; Daisy Miller turning, via Natalie Wood, into Marjorie Morningstar) took its place. Granted, this is to talk about a vulgar inheritance rather than an authentic one. It is to talk about the stock features of Borsht Belt comedy: Jewish momma jokes, gefilte fish and the *shmaltz* of fading memories dished up generously in cocktail lounges.

Moreover, that Dream Factory we call Hollywood had its effects, especially where such comedy was concerned. The "tall tale"—so much a part of the frontier sensibility—gave way to more urban, which is to say, "Jewish" forms. Prototypes of the schlemiel flourished in one-reelers and, later, in popular culture itself. Sacred cows were regularly led to gleeful slaughter and ironic reversals of all stripes became the order of the day. The technique is, after all, simple enough: merely turn life upside-down and shake. Soon the whole country became experts in the art. Even the irreverent humor of "Laugh-In" or the delicately poised satire of "All in the Family" could pile up big ratings in the Heartland.

Ironically enough, these curious juxtapositions created special problems for the post-war American-Jewish writer. Literary sociologists are fond of mentioning the Second World War as that trauma which reversed the gradual drift toward total assimilation. Perhaps.   .   . and, yet, the most significant Holocaust literature has been written by Europeans like Andre Swartz-Bart (*The Last Of The Just*) or Elie Wiesel (*Night, Dawn*). The lack of first-hand experience accounts for some of the reluctance to give the grotesque dimensions of the Holocaust a literary pattern, but there were historical reasons on the New York side of the Atlantic as well. The American-Jewish writer was simply caught off-base by the cunning of history, his head too filled with tag lines from Eliot and the *Partisan Review*. Denied a comfortable identity as a Jew in America, he went about the business of *creating* one. After all, in the twenties serious literature had been *of* him and possibly even *for* him, but hardly ever *by* him. This time the American-Jewish writer vowed it would all be different. The fortunes of Faulkner & Co. were on the skids and while the literary South might rise again, the mainstream had shifted to the city. In short, the journals, the critics and a generation of eager, young American-Jewish writers made the mix seem just about right.

But the growth of what came to be known as the American-Jewish literary Mafioso never seemed quite kosher. It appeared as if a metaphorical plot had been abrew, the editors of *Commentary* magazine hatching the whole thing up in some East Side delicatessen. Robert Alter—ironically enough, writing in *Commentary*— put it this way:

> .   .   . when a writer assigns a set of abstract moral values to the representatives of a particular group, the connection thus insisted on may strike the reader as arbitrary, an artistic confusion of actualities and ideals.[2]

The Fifties learned to speak with a literary patois that slipped into quasi-Yiddish at the drop of a whitefish. Characters who "suffered" appeared breathlessly from some off-stage nowhere, as if they had just changed clothes from a four-thousand year trek across the desert. A prolonged sigh or nonverbal grunt was enough to insure character credibility, even depth. Nobody was particularly surprised when the future of such fiction was declared "doubtful."

In fact, during the Fifties one began to yearn for those Aristotelian days when literary movements in America had definable beginnings, middles and, best of all, *ends*. Critics talked about the Twenties or the Thirties or even the Forties as if our society and its literature had been arranged neatly by decades. And for good reasons. The stock market had crashed (conveniently enough) in 1929 and suddenly the "jazz age" no longer seemed an appropriate metaphor of the country's mood. Ten years later the Stalin-Hitler pact and the outbreak of World War II had a similarly foreclosing effect on the 1930's.

But history has a way of happening independently, without the advice or consent of literary scholars. Weighty events occur willy-nilly, as often in the middle of decades as at either end. All this tends to create unfortunate side-effects, particularly when the old classifications are concerned. To be sure, the "decade" may have *always* been a decidely limited yardstick. And, yet, in the Fifties it became increasingly clear that literary movements not only refused to die on schedule, but some of them refused to die at all.

American-Jewish literature is probably the most striking example of this phenomenon. Critics in the late Fifties hovered over the would-be corpse while visions of obituary danced in their heads—only to discover the patient lingering endlessly between one bowl of watered-down chicken soup and the next. Just when it looked, at least to some, as if the tragi-comic condition of the American Jew had been exhausted totally, a 26 year-old author named Philip Roth sent the critics scurrying to their typewriters once again. *Commentary*—which had published "Eli, the Fanatic" some two years earlier—crackled with an avalanche of pro and con. To be sure, there had been Jewish satirists before. Mendele the Bookseller exposed the corruption and folly of shtetl life with the savagery of a Swift. And, the Prophets did not hesitate to throw a well-aimed stone at the Establishment when they felt the urge, Divine or otherwise. But *Goodbye, Columbus*, so the argument went, was another story altogether. It is one thing to criticize and quite another to mock from an aesthetic distance. Besides, Mendele wrote in Yiddish; *his* barbs remained an internal affair. With Philip Roth, however, the dirty linen hung from all too public lines. What would the *goyim* think when they read such unpleasant stuff in the pages of, say, the *New Yorker*?

Historians of the future will be hard pressed to account for the literary prominence of Newark, New Jersey. Perhaps it is mere conincidence that such influential figures as Leslie Fiedler, LeRoi Jones and Philip Roth were nurtured there. Perhaps not. After all, that an Ezra Pound should come from Haley, Idaho, a T. S. Eliot from St. Louis, Missouri or an Ernest Hemingway from Oak Park, Illinois, no longer seems surprising. The very provinciality of such Midwestern soil was just what a rebellious movement like Modernism required. At least *some* of their respective energy mounted against philistinism can be chalked up to overcompensation.

But no such common threads unite Fiedler, Roth and Jones. Fiedler—always more the Post-Modernist than he had imagined— charted his course Westward, to that place in myth where red men are really black men (or is it the other way around?) and *all men*, at bottom, are Jews. LeRoi Jones, on the other hand, has metamorphosed himself into Imamu Baraka, a son of Africa rather than Newark. Only Roth seems inextricably tied to the apronstrings of New Jersey, no matter how hard he tries to shift his locale to the Gentile Midwest. Like Joyce's notion of "dear, dirty Dublin," Newark and its environs keep both the adrenalin and the fictional juices running strong.

There is a good deal of common ground between, say, James Joyce's *Dubliners* and the stories of Philip Roth's *Goodbye, Columbus*. Both are out to expose the pettiness and vulgarity of a provincial, limiting life. But the parallels soon disappear. Stephen Dedalus may be trying to awaken from that nightmare which is history, to fly over those nets of paralysis called family, church and state, but at least he has a viable heritage to renounce. Roth, on the other hand, has no substructure left to attack, no battles remaining to be fought. He begins, in effect, at the *end* of an identifiable American-Jewish experience, at a moment in history when one can choose to be—or not to be—"Jewish."

At a point midway in the 1960's Leslie Fiedler suggested that:

> . . . the moment of triumph for the Jewish writer in the United
> States has come just when his awareness of himself as a Jew is reaching
> a vanishing point, when the gesture of rejection seems his last possible
> connection with his historical past; and the popular acceptance of his
> alienation threatens to turn into an affectation, a fashionable cliché.
> (p. 66)

Neither the free-thinking Jew nor the religiously devout one could
have imagined such a radical change in less than three generations.
Their quarrels—for all the pyrotechnics—had the look of a family
spat. Feelings ran high, of course, but when somebody on the lower
East Side declared that "All men are Jews," it had a very different
ring than it does in Bernard Malamud. In short, about *some* defini-
tions there was a consensus and, more important, a willingness to
accept at least the broad outlines of a common heritage. By contrast, Roth seemed to be the wicked son of the Passover story,
forever asking: "Why do *you* (rather than the collective "we")
celebrate these things?"

Neil Klugman, the protagonist of "Goodbye, Columbus,"
has that pissed-off, vaguely artsy look of a Jack Nicholson
character, although it was Richard Benjamin, "alone and palely
loitering" among those richer Jews of the country club set, who
won the role. I mention this, not in the spirit of a film buff's one-
upsmanship, but, rather, as one who savors his puns. As any number
of Yiddishists—both "professional" and strictly amateur—have
pointed out, "Klugman" is an ingenious bit of wordplay, one
which combines the Yiddish adjective for "clever" with an anagram
of the Yiddish noun ("Klog") suggesting "curse." Interestingly
enough, one popular Yiddish curse (see Michael Gold's *Jews
Without Money*) was *"a klog af Columbus!"* (A curse on
Columbus). As the inflated expectations immigrant Jews had about
that "Golden Land" called America began to turn sour, such sentiments increased in frequency. Roth, I hasten to add, is quick to
affirm his ignorance of Yiddish—beyond, say, those idiomatic expressions one hears on the Johnny Carson Show—and I would be
quick to agree.

Still, the combination of wit and curse is evident enough in
Klugman. The story itself is one of class struggle—the HAVES of
Short Hills vs. the HAVE-NOTS of Newark, quasi-WASP against
left-over Jew. That Ali McGraw should play Brenda Patimkin makes

for delicious ironies all their own, rather like Erich Segal dreaming
of himself as Ryan O'Neil in *Love Story*. The following juxtaposi-
tion suggests the broad-ax way food serves to define the respective
teams:

THE KLUGMAN CLAN

. . . —pepper wasn't served in her home; she'd heard on Galen Drake
that it was not absorbed by the body, and it was distrubing to Aunt
Gladys to think that anything she served might pass through a gullet,
stomach, and bowel just for the pleasure of the trip.

'You're going to pick the peas out is all? You tell me that, I
wouldn't buy with the carrots.'

'I love carrots,' I said, 'I love them.' And to prove it, I dumpled
half of them down my throat and the other half onto my trousers.

'Pig,' she said. [3] (p. 6)

.   .   .   .

THE PATIMKIN GROUP

I opened the door of the old refrigerator; it was not empty. No
longer did it hold butter, eggs, herring in cream sauce, ginger ale, tuna
fish salad, an occasional corsage—rather it was heaped with fruit,
shelves swelled with it, every color, every texture, and hidden within,
every kind of pit. There were greengage plums, black plums, red plums,
apricots, nectarines, peaches, long horns of grapes, black, yellow, red,
and cherries, cherries flowing out of boxes and staining everything
scarlet. And there were melons—cantelopes and honeydews—and on
the top shelf, half of a huge watermelon, a thin sheet of wax paper
clinging to its bare red face like a wet lip. Oh Patimkim! Fruit grew in
their refrigerator and sporting goods dropped from their trees. (p. 43)

The Patimkin refrigerator—a haunting reminder of less prosperous
days in Newark—seems more akin to the world of Andrew Marvell's
"The Garden" than a gameroom in Short Hills. And, indeed, all the
"nectarine (s) and curious peach (es)" suggest a kind of gastronomic
Eden, one whose lushness ensnares Klugman in much the same way

it affected Marvell's protagonist.

Eden, however, has a number of conflicting faces in "Good-bye, Columbus." For Klugman's alter-ego—a small Negro boy who makes daily pilgrimages to the library—it is a book of reproductions by Gauguin. As he imagines it, such a Tahitian paradise constitutes "the fuckin' life." The boy functions as a point of reference for Klugman, especially when more conspicuous sport threatens to become unbearable.

Moreover, the Negro boy's alternating bravado and uneasiness at the library is a mirror image of Klugman's own behavior at the Patimkin's. The fusion is achieved, symbolically enough, in a myth-opoeic dream which looks as if it had just stepped out of a page from Leslie Fiedler's *Love And Death In The American Novel*:

> I touched her in my sleep, for the dream had unsettled me: it had taken place on a ship, an old sailing ship like those you see in pirate movies. With me on the ship was the little colored kid from the library—I was the captain and he my mate, and we were the only crew members. For a while it was a pleasant dream; we were anchored in the harbor of an island in the Pacific and it was very sunny. Upon the beach there were beautiful bare-skinned Negresses, and none of them moved. But suddenly *we* were moving, our ship, out of the harbor, and the Negresses moved slowly down to the shore and began to throw leis at us and say 'Goodbye, Columbus. . . goodbye. . .' and though we did not want to go, the little boy and I, the boat was moving and there was nothing we could do about it, and he shouted at me that it was my fault and I shouted it was his for not having a library card, but we were wasting our breath, for we were further and further from the island, and soon the natives were nothing at all. (p. 74)

Of course Klugman's fantasy is not *quite* Huck and Jim on the raft or Ishmael and Queequeg on the whaler; rather, it is a foreshadowing of Eden inverted, the Short Hills that, for Klugman, ever recede.

Such high-brow analysis begs the more obvious sociological point. *Goodbye, Columbus* won its notoriety on the same dreary grounds that had plagued American-literature since its beginnings. In 1917 Abraham Cahan's unflattering portrait of the unscupulous David Levinsky had drawn charges of "Foul!" from the official Jewish Establishment. Roth also had an abrasive habit of hitting on

sensitive nerves. If Cahan fancied himself a "muckraker," Roth was
out to be the Evelyn Waugh of American-Jewish letters, one eye
always open for the undercutting detail:

> Also there were Mrs. Patimkin's twin sisters, Rose and Pearl, who
> both had white hair, the color of Lincoln convertibles and nasal voices,
> and husbands who followed after them but talked only to each other,
> as though, in fact, sister had married sister, and husband had married
> husband. The husbands, named Earl Klein and Manny Kartzman, sat
> next to each other during the ceremony, then after dinner, and once,
> in fact, while the band was playing in between courses, they rose,
> Klein and Kartzman, as though to dance, but instead walked to the
> far end of the hall where together they paced off the width of the floor.
> Earl, I learned later, was in the carpet business, and apparently he was
> trying to figure how much money he would make if the Hotel Pierre
> favored him with a sale. (pp. 106-107)

"Goodbye, Columbus" picks on relatively easy targets—
Jewish weddings, the B'nai Brith, suburbia in general— and, in the
process, Roth took some cheap shots:

> 'We're all going to Temple Friday night. Why don't you come
> with us? I mean, are you orthodox or conservative?'

> I considered. 'Well, I haven't gone in a long time.   . . I'm just
> Jewish,' I said well-meaningly, but that too sent Mrs. Patimkin back
> to her Hadassah work. Desperately I tried to think of something that
> would convince her I wasn't an infidel. Finally I asked: 'Do you know
> Martin Buber's work?'

> 'Buber.   .   . Buber,' she asked, looking at her Hadassah list. 'Is
> he orthodox or conservative?' she asked.

> 'He's a philosopher.'

> 'Is he reformed?' she asked, piqued either at the possibility
> that Buber attended Friday night services without a hat, or Mrs. Buber
> had only one set of dishes in her kitchen.

> 'Orthodox,' I said faintly.

> 'That's very nice,' she said. (p. 88)

The clash of American-Jewish life styles—Klugman new
English versus Patimkin new money—provides the satiric backdrop

against which the love story of Brenda and Neil can be played. The college girl may have entered the literary scene from stage South—as Temple Drake or some avatar of Zelda Sayre—but it was Marjorie Morningstar, Franny Glass and, finally, Brenda Patimkin who became the apotheosis of the form. Doris Klugman plows her way through *War and Peace* in the summer; Brenda, only half-joking, claims to have grown a penis. Roth can catalogue the vulgarities of Short Hills' life with the wry contempt of a solid outsider, but the Jewish Princess-as-Bitch has a way of shrinking his aesthetic distance to a bare minimum. As Neil puts it:

> We were dressed similarly, sneakers, sweat socks, khaki Bermudas, and sweat shirts, but I had the feeling that Brenda was not talking about the accidents of our dress—if they were accidents. She meant, I was sure, that I was somehow beginning to look the way she wanted me to. Like herself. (p. 70)

Much of "Goodbye, Columbus" rests of such parlor Freud, including the "accidental" discovery of Brenda's diaphragm and the subsequent Neil-Brenda breakup. Klugman's final bit of tough guy bravado—"I did not look very much longer, but took the train that got into Newark just as the sun was rising on the first day of the Jewish New Year. I was back in plenty of time for work."—smacks of imitation Hemingway. At last the sun also rises for nice Jewish boys.

With the exception of "You Can't Tell a Man by the Song He Sings"—a fairly heavy-handed allegory about Joseph McCarthyism—the remaining stories in Roth's first collection continue to probe the American-Jewish psyche. In "Eli, the Fanatic" (easily the best story in *Goodbye, Columbus*), the tension between memories of a shtetl past and an assimilated present produces a nearly perfect fictional balance. Eli Peck comes to the confrontation armed with zoning ordinances and a law degree. Leo Tzuref, on the other hand, defends his yeshivah with Talmudic reasoning and the exotic trappings of Hassidic Jewry. The story deals with such familiar themes as conformity, materialism and fashionable breakdown, but, this time, Roth comes at them from the oblique angle of myth. Tzuref, after all, is hardly a *realistic* portrait of the Hassid. The laws of *shatnais* (which deal with forbidden blends of fiber), as well as the value Hassidim place on their time-honored clothing cannot help but make all the suit-switching in "Eli, the Fanatic" look a bit silly. Roth, it is clear, has not done his Sunday School home-work. However, the quasi-Shakespearean quality of the costume changes strikes us as *aesthetically* right. For Peck, the Hassid is an index of a more meaningful past, one which stands in dramatic counterpoint to the Ivy-League world of Eli, the lawyer. And his final, desperate substitution compels the movement to that ambig-uous level of myth where madness and clear vision remain sus-pended.

A similar progress occurs in the dream-like world of "The Conversion of the Jews." Oscar Freedman (a prototype of Alexander Portnoys to come) is struck, again and again, by the con-tradictions which separate the humanitarian from the parochial Jew:

> Then there was the plane crash. Fifty-eight people had been killed in a plane crash at La Guardia. In studying a casualty list in the newspapers his mother had discovered among the list of those dead eight Jewish names (his grandmother had nine but she counted Miller as a Jewish name); because of the eight she said the plane crash was "a tragedy." During free-discussion time on Wednesday Ozzie had brought to Rabbi Binder's attention this matter of "some of his relations" always picking out the Jewish names. Rabbi Binder had begun to explain cultural unity and some other things when Ozzie stood up at his seat and said what he wanted to know was different. Rabbi Binder insisted that he sit down. . . (p. 141-142)

However, when Ozzie's questions—about the possibility of a virgin birth or the logic of calling Jews the "Chosen People"—finally reach a crescendo, the realistic trappings fall away and the story moves into a world of Biblical fantasy reconstituted:

> 'Momma.'
>
> 'Yes, Oscar.'
>
> 'Momma, get down on your knees, like Rabbi Binder.'
>
> 'Oscar—'
>
> 'Get down on your knees or I'll jump.' Oscar heard a whimper, then a quick rustling and when he looked down where his mother had stood he saw the top of a head and beneath that a circle of dress. She was kneeling beside Rabbi Binder.

> He spoke again. 'Everybody kneel.' There was the sound of everybody kneeling. . .

> Next, Ozzie made everybody say it (i.e. that God could make a child without intercourse). And then he made them all say they believed in Jesus Christ—first one at a time, then all together. (p. 156-157)

Ozzie, of course, is an ironic Joseph, one whose dreams have a distinctly Freudian cast. All the forces of the super-ego are represented—preacher, teacher, fireman, cop—and Ozzie's wish fulfillment wins the day. The Jews are "converted" and, for the moment at least, authoritarian roles are reversed.

But such dreams are made of fragile stuff and the built-in victories, however sweeping, do not last. "Defender of the Faith," for example, makes for an interesting counterpoint, one which looks at the anguish of authority from the other side of the coin. The story has been widely misread as a self-hating—and grossly unfair—portrait of Jewish soldiers, just the sort of thing that could turn the average *New Yorker* reader into an anti-Semite. Only "Epstein" (about a Jewish "adulterer" no less!) seems more patently unfair to official guardians of the official morality. After all, the argument went, there *were* Jewish war heroes, but never Jewish adulterers. At least that is the vision of American-Jewish life as PR men would have it, complete to the one Jewish G.I. (Orthodox and stubbornly observant even in battle), whose presence in the microcosmic platoon was as predictable as his death by the end of the third reel. Neither Grossbart nor Fishbein, however, are the "defenders of the faith," for all their whining about Jewish rights. Rather, it is Sergeant Marx—a Jewish war hero of the John Wayne stripe—who discovers, first, the vulnerability and then the anguish which comes with a recognition of his roots. To Grossbart and Fishbein, Marx's "Jewishness" is a reservoir of vague guilts that can be tapped for special considerations. Goldbrickism becomes the order of the day. But to admit one's identity (as Marx must) is only half the story. The other side of the sergeant's coin allows for perspective and that dovetailing of professional responsibility and personal freedom he calls "fate."

Ten years after the publication of *Goodbye, Columbus*—following side excursions to Chicago (*Letting Go*, 1962) and the Gentile Mid-West (*When She Was Good*, 1966)—Roth returned to Newark and the second installment of his serio-comic quarrel with childhood roots. Parts of it had already appeared in *New American Review, Partisan Review* and *Esquire*. Publicity about it appeared everywhere: on talk shows, in newspapers and, of course, at indignant synagogues. The advance sales were staggering; rumors about what Hollywood was willing to pay for the rights dazzled serious authors and critics alike. It was 1969 and the decade seemed a sure bet to end with a literary bang. The book, of course, was *Portnoy's Complaint*.

But "sensation" has a nasty habit of leading us astray—to tedious discussions about pornography, self-hatred or whether serious Art and high profits can co-exist. In all the frenzy the book itself can, and often *does*, get lost. *Portnoy's Complaint* is a prolonged *kvetch* (in English, read "complaint"), one nervously anchored to the analyst's couch. Unlike *Letting Go* or *When She Was Good*, this time it is the stand-up comedian (rather than Henry James or Gustave Flaubert) whose "influence" makes the difference. And this is particularly true in the book's very rhythm, its "blends" from one comic bit to another. To be sure, literary allusions are generously sprinkled throughout (*King Lear*, "Leda and the Swan," Kafka and, of course, *Oedipus Rex*), but it is the unlikely combination of a Myron Cohen and a Lenny Bruce which gives the monologue its forward motion. Not since Salinger's *The Catcher In The Rye* had a novel been so readable, so "right" for its time and place. It was urban, hip, swinging, irreverent, cutely neurotic and all the rest. And not since Salinger had so many readers identified with a character so deeply. Holden Caulfield was the perfect emblem of the innocent Fifties; Alexander Portnoy threatened to become a similar cause celebre for the permissive Sixties.

Such a book, then, is extremely hard to pin down. The very title, for example, works on at least three levels: it is a "complaint" in the legalistic sense of the word—an indictment handed down against those cultural forces which have created him; it is a "complaint" in the old-fashioned sense of illness, one Dr. Spielvogel comically describes in clinical language as "A distortion in which strongly-felt ethical and altruistic impulses are perpetually warring with extreme sexual longings, often of a perverse nature."; and, finally, it is a "complaint" in the melancholy lover's sense of the term.

Alexander Portnoy—who is, significantly enough, both thirty-three years old and New York City's Assistant Commissioner of Human Opportunity—finds himself at psychological loose-ends when the novel begins. That his age is the same as Christ when crucified, that he protects the sacredness of every human opportunity except, presumably, his own, makes for intriguing possibilities. But *that*, it seems to me, is exactly the problem: *Portnoy's Complaint* is as filled with "possibilities" as it is riddled by "contradictions." Portnoy would, no doubt, agree with the speaker of Walt Whitman's "Song of Myself":

> Do I contradict myself?
>
> Very well then I contradict myself.
>
> (I am large, I contain multitudes)

The difference, of course, is that Whitman's poem is a hairy-chested celebration of his cosmic—which is to say, largely imagined—Selfhood, while Portnoy's systematic contradictions are the very stuff of "confession."

In this sense Portnoy is closer to Leopold Bloom, the multi-faceted protagonist of Joyce's *Ulysses*. In the very jumble of personality traits, the alternating currents of love and hatred, Portnoy is the Protean teller of his own tragi-comic tale. The book is both an extended confessional (albeit, of a comically outrageous stripe) and an attempt at exorcism. But while Portnoy shares much of the fading Jewishness which defines a Bloom, their respective contexts are very different indeed. To be a Jew in Dublin is to be a walking contradiction, a joke *a priori*. Portnoy, on the other hand, grows up in that uneasy limbo between total assimilation and authentic Jewishness called Newark. Even *he* often has trouble distinguishing the "truth" behind his compulsive needs to complain, to confess, to project guilt, to wallow in self-hatred:

> All I do is complain, the repugnance seems bottomless, and I'm beginning to wonder if maybe enough isn't enough. I hear myself indulging in the kind of ritualized bellyaching that is just what gives psychoanalytic patients such a bad name with the general public. Could I really have detested this childhood and resented these poor parents of mine to the same degree then that I seem to now, looking backward

upon what I was from the vantage point of what I am—and am not?
Is this the truth I'm delivering up, or is it just plain *kvetching?* Or
is kvetching for people like me a *form* of truth? [4]   (pp. 93-94)

Granted, Portnoy's fractured monologue comes all in a rush, as if
repression had made it impossible to talk about these matters before. Still, his kvetching *is* a *"form* of truth," especially if one sees
it as the essential truth grossly distorted for comic effect. Portnoy's
self-lacerating wit bears at least some relationship to traditional
Jewish humor, particularly where the dynamics of beating a hostile
world to the punch are concerned. He undercuts himself with a
relish that only those thoroughly infected with that sensibility we
now call Black Humor can understand. Fantasy is its staple. In
Portnoy's case, the elusive truth is a mixture of actual event and
what the imagination can make of it. Recurrent fears express themselves as fantasized headlines in the *Daily News* or in comic bits
projected on the mind's inner screen.

For Roth, it made for a congenial, even distinctive style of
writing: what wowed them at last night's cocktail party became the
raw material of a next morning's work. Sustaining a "voice"
throughout—a matter of refining language until it had the *illusion* of
colloquial speech—may account for the book's enormous success
and the movie version's dismal failure. In *print*, as it were, even
Portnoy's wildest, most obscene ranting has an appeal which is
totally lost when transferred to another medium.

Portnoy has a monopoly on the analyst's couch—which, in
this case, turns out to be center stage. Others are relegated to sec-
ondary positions as straw men in the shifting chronology of
Portnoy's memories. But one soon begins to suspect that Portnoy
complaineth *too* much, that there is another side to his psycho-
logically crippled coin we are not hearing. At first glance the novel
encourages easy identification—"Portnoy is *moi!*" many readers
were heard to shout—unaware that subtlties of tone may, in fact,
be undercutting their "hero" at every turn. Others insisted that the
whole Jewish Momma/Jewish son business was neither aesthetically
interesting nor ethnically indigenous. After all, Italian mothers (or
Russian ones or whatever) had many of the same characteristics.
And, finally, there were those who dismissed the portraits as patently unfair; for them nothing substantial had changed between
Goodbye, Columbus and *Portnoy's Complaint*—except that the
latest travesty was even "dirtier."

Portnoy begins his *shpiel* to Dr. Spielvogel with a sketch entitled "The Most Unforgettable Character I've Met." However, unlike the uplifting stories which appear under that rubric in *Reader's Digest,* Portnoy's version is darkly Freudian, an introduction to those psychological determiners who have, in effect, put him on the couch. His mother, Sophie Portnoy—more Borsht Belt fantasy than actual person—is the prime stinker in this self-constructed Rorschach. As the capital-S Super-ego, she was "so imbedded in my consciousness that for the first year of school I seem to have believed that each of my teachers was my mother in disguise." And, too, she is the Jewish mother joke incarnate, full of sardonic, but ultimately castrating wit:

> Of my sallow, overweight older sister, my mother would say (in Hannah's presence, of course: honesty was her policy too), 'The child is no genius, but then we don't ask the impossible. God bless her, she works hard, she applies herself to her limits, and so whatever she gets is all right.' Of me, the heir to her long Egyptian nose and clever babbling mouth, of me my mother would say, with characteristic restraint, 'This *bonditt*? He doesn't even have to open a book—'A' in everything. Albert Einstein the Second.' (p. 2)

It is Sophie, of course, who looms over the terrified Alex "with a long bread knife in her hands" and who locks him out of the apartment when he is "bad." She is, in short, that double-faced figure of the Mother (one aspect of her nurturing, the other devouring) outlined in anthopological studies like Robert Graves' *The White Goddess.* Most of all, she is "thorough":

> For mistakes she checked my sums; for holes, my socks; for dirt, my nails, my neck, every seam and crease of my body. She even dredges the furtherest recesses of my ears by pouring cold peroxide into my head. It tingles and pops like an earful of ginger ale, and brings to the surface, in bits and pieces, the hidden stores of yellow wax, which can apparently endanger a person's hearing. (p. 10)

Fears about the body's health—and their resulting, largely superstitious remedies—are the legacy Portnoy both rebels against and cannot quite manage to shake. Given the omnipotent Matriarch Sophie is, Alex seems driven to assert his masculinity in all the grotesqueness of overcompensation. But *real* power (as Sophie knows unconsciously, without the benefit of articles in *Partisan Review*) is confident, unquestioning, sure of itself. Comic ambivalence may make Alex an attractive narrator to those afflicted with the same malady, but it is the *un*examined life which wields the novel's psychological sticks. As Melvin Friedman has pointed out: "Alexander Portnoy requires psychiatric help, not his Jewish mother." [5]

Portnoy's father, on the other hand, provides a poignant model of all his son hysterically seeks to avoid. As Jack Portnoy's comic version of the Cartesian formula would have it: "I am repressed or castrated or whatever; therefore, I am constipated":

> He drank—of course, not whiskey like a *goy*, but mineral oil and milk of magnesia; and chewed on Ex-Lax; and ate All-Bran morning and night; and downed mixed fruit by the pound bag. He suffered—did he suffer!—from constipation. . . . He used to brew senna leaves in a saucepan, and that, along with the suppository melting invisibly in his rectum, comprised *his* witchcraft. . . . But all catharses were in vain for that man: his *kishkes* were gripped by the iron hand of outrage and frustration. Among his other misfortunes, I was his wife's favorite. (pp. 2-3)

Significantly enough, he is an insurance salesman, peddling the promise of security (an "umbrella for a rainy day") to everyone but himself. Long-suffering—as Sophie is constantly tormenting—Portnoy's father is the grumbling Stoic, a man resigned to his inevitable fate as an American-Jewish father. He *provides*, but can himself find no relief.

Portnoy's Complaint shares much with books like D. H. Lawrence's *Sons And Lovers* or Joyce's *A Portrait Of The Artist As A Young Man*. They are all examples of the bildungsroman, novels which chronicle the growth and "education" of a sensitive, young protagonist. That the Oedipal complex which so tortured Lawrence's Paul Morel (who is both "son" *and* "lover") is shared by Alexander Portnoy seems as obvious as it is, ultimately, misleading. In a general sense Lawrence's novel is the prototype of those preoccupations which seem to characterize American—Jewish fiction: Freudian hatred of the father; obsessive love by and for the mother. But for all Portnoy's insistence that this is the alpha and omega of his malady, socio-economic factors—as opposed to purely Freudian ones—also play a significant role. Portnoy belongs to that culture of sons for which some two generations of immigrant Jewish parents worked. As Portnoy himself puts it:

> Where he had been imprisoned, I would fly; that was his dream. Mine was the corollary: in my liberation would be his—from ignorance, from anonymity. To this day our destinies remain scrambled together in my imagination, and there are still too many times when, upon reading in some book a passage that impresses me with its logic or its wisdom, instantly, involuntarily, I think, 'If only he could read *this*. Yes! Read, and understand—!' (p. 7)

In effect, Portnoy is a scorecard of both the assets and liabilities of such a program. Groomed to "succeed," Portnoy has. But what Norman Podhoretz calls the "small-print costs" of such success are also there.[6] The curiously intertwining love and hatred *he* feels is, no doubt, matched by similar emotions on the other side of the generational coin. Portnoy's swinging idiom is, in that sense, not very far removed from that of his parents. What the former says with bile, the latter say with *shmaltz.*

It is easy enough to heap criticism on their programatic attempts to restrict his manhood, keep him, forever, the terrified little boy seeking praise and fearing punishment. It is easy enough to rail at "this schmuck, this moron, this Philistine father of mine!" whose crime, in this case, was to throw away *Partisan Review* un-read. But such adolescent postures (Why can't my parents be more like my professors? My favorite author? Me?) begin to cloy at thirty-three. After all, Jack Portnoy no doubt picked up the rather considerable tab for his son's education. But Alex, like Stephen Dedalus, wants no truck with anything less than High Art. And like the priggish Stephen, Alex "will not serve" those false idols in which he no longer believes:

> But I am something more, or so they tell me. A Jew. No! No! An *atheist*, I cry. I am a nothing where religion is concerned, and I will not pretend to be anything that I am not! I don't care how lonely and needy my father is, the truth about me is the truth about me, and I'm sorry but he'll have to swallow my apostasy whole! .   . .(p. 71)

Stephen, of course, meets Leopold Bloom and learns those lessons about humanity and the human heart which such self-styled intel-lectuals too often overlook. Alexander Portnoy, alas, has no such instructor. However, he really doesn't *want* one. His prolonged confession and/or complaint has a self-indulgent quality about it, as if it had already become a comfortable script. And so, Portnoy conveniently arranges the chronology, embellishing twice-told tales with guilt or blame until the result is an illusion of discovery.

But the cards have been well stacked beforehand—and life inside his particular Jewish joke at least preserves a capacity for control. That he can *talk* so glibly about masturbation, impotence and a laundry-list of perversions (both real and imagined) in between suggests the differences between this book and those of Lawrence and Joyce. What they took with high seriousness Roth reduces to the merely flip. Cultural history may be the real villain here. That is, when Portnoy shouts "LET'S PUT THE ID BACK IN YID" the effect dilutes the now familiar Freudian jargon into the jazzy stuff of pop culture. Critics desperate for psychoanalytic patterns can find God's plenty, but it is the context—rather than the "substance"—which is probably more important.

What the novel is fact provides in an encyclopedia of moments drawn from an American-Jewish ethos in its final, most vulgar, phase. One axiom strikes me as particularly relevant here: when a Tradition begins to question itself, it is, in large measure, already in a stage of serious decline. Portnoy comes at the ragged end of a culture that had sustained itself with dignity and now cannot. What he sees, of course, is the residue of a superstructure (ethnic indicators like "real Jewish jello" or mah-jong), rather than its more meaningful substructure. In a book which militates against a complexity of characterization (substituting, instead, the stock figures of the skit-and-blackout) precious little gets mounted up to sidetract Portnoy's sweeping condemnations. At one point, however, his father asks:

> 'Tell me something, do you know Talmud, my educated son? Do you know history? One-two-three you were bar mitzvah, and that for you was the end of your religious education. Do you know men study their whole lives in the Jewish religion, and when they die they still haven't finished? Tell me, now that you are finished at fourteen being a Jew, do you know a single thing about the wonderful history and heritage of the saga of your people?' (p. 61)

Fair questions all, although Jack Portnoy may not be the best person to ask them. For him, the "saga of the Jews" is as much a cliché as are the terms of Portnoy's rebuttal. As Irving Howe has suggested, what Portnoy expresses is "the wish to sever his sexuality from his moral responsibilities, to cut it away from his self as historical creature." [7] The result may be a "castration" even more fearful than the one Sophie signifies. To live in a historical anonymity might be a currently fashionable dream, but it is no less foolish thereby. Portnoy is the most notorious spokesman for the special brands of schizophrenia and blindness that are by-products of such a "liberated" life. Even his ringing claim that "I am a human being!" waxes meaningless without a cultural context.

This much said, however, one must turn to that vulgarization of a "cultural context" which is Portnoy's unhappy lot. It is largely defined by an assortment of "Thou Shalt Not's!", some originating on Sinai, but most from Sophie Portnoy herself. Jewish people, Portnoy soon discovers, do not "believe" in (a) Christmas (b) athletics in general (c) French fries (d) baton-twirling (e) hunting, etc. etc. At one point in his relentless attack on such a mentality, Portnoy remembers that, as a small child, he had "turned from the window out of which I was watching a snowstorm and hopefully asked 'Momma, do we believe in winter?'" In the Portnoy household the world divides neatly into that which is "Jewish" and the rest which is "goyische":

> Because I am sick and tired of *goyische* this and *goyische* that! If it's bad it's the *goyim*, if it's good it's the Jews! Can't you see, my dear parents, from whose loins I somehow leaped, that such thinking is a trifle barbaric? That all you are expressing is your *fear*? The very first distinction I learned from you, I'm sure, was not night and day, or hot and cold, but *goyische* and Jewish! (p. 74)

Portnoy responds to such indoctrination with a solipsistic vengeance. And in that lonely world where he, alone, is a "human being," he alternates between castigating the Gentiles (*"Americans—* like Henry Aldrich and Homer, like the Great Gildersleeve and his nephew LeRoy, like Corliss and Veronica, like 'Oogie Pringle' who gets to sing beneath Jane Powell's window in *A Date with Judy—* these are the people for whom Nat 'King' Cole sings every Christmastime, 'Chestnuts roasting on an open fire, Jack Frost nipping at your nose' ") and berating the Jews ("The guilt, the fears—the terror bred into my bones! What in their world was not charged with danger, dripping with germs, fraught with peril?"). Rampant sexuality (not since Lawrence at his wackiest has there been such a prolonged phallic consciousness) becomes his weapon in an unending war against instilled repression and neurotic fears about the body's function. At first glance "impotence" seems exactly the *wrong* word to describe Portnoy's chaotic sexual behavior.

From the imaginary Thereal McCoy of his adolescent fantasies at
the Empire Burlesque House through his sordid history of private
masturbations, semi-public displays on the 107 bus and the wildly
comic assist provided by a Bubbles Girardi to his pornographic
dreams realized in Mary Jane Reed (the Monkey), Portnoy appears
more hyper-active than ineffectual. Freud's seminal essay "The
Most Prevalent Form of Degradation in Erotic Life" (which Roth
borrows as the title for a chapter about Portnoy's ill-fated love
affairs) provides a kind of partial answer: "Where such men love
they have no desire   [suggests the good Viennese Docktor] , and
where they desire they cannot love." The underlying cause is, of
course, the Oedipal complex; an obsessive love for the mother turns
eligible women into either competing Madonnas (who, like the
Oedipal Mother, are protected from carnality by the force of taboo)
or prostitutes with whom one may lust but never "love." As
Portnoy reviews the respective cases of The Monkey, Kay Campbell
(The "Pumpkin") and Sarah Abbot Maulsby (The "Pilgrim"), the
warnings of his mother (hysterical, capitalized even!) ring in his
ears:

> DON'T RUN FIRST THING TO A BLONDIE, *PLEASE*! BECAUSE
> SHE'LL TAKE   YOU   FOR ALL YOU'RE WORTH   AND   THEN
> LEAVE YOU BLEADING (sic) IN THE GUTTER! A BRILLIANT
> INNOCENT BABY BOY LIKE YOU, SHE'LL EAT YOU UP ALIVE!
> (p. 188)

For all the dirty jokes and Freudian puns Portnoy can make about
such remarks, deep-seated guilts are never far from pornographic
pleasure. In the case of The Monkey, an illiterate note to her
cleaning lady is the last straw:

> dir willa polish the flor by bathrum *pleze* & dont furget the insies of
> windose mary jane r (p. 205)

Even the notorious Molly Bloom did not make such glaring errors—
and, interestingly enough, they *matter* to Portnoy. Professional defender of the downtrodden, Portnoy is, nonetheless, an intellectual
snob:

> What was I thinking about in Vermont! Of that z, that z between the
> two e's of 'pleze'—this is a mind with the depths of a movie marquee!
> And 'furget'! Exactly how a prostitute would misspell that word!
> But it's something about the mangling of 'dear,' that tender syllable

of affection now collapsed into three lower-case letters, that strikes me as hopelessly pathetic. How unnatural can a relationship be! This woman is ineducable and beyond reclamation. By contrast to hers, my childhood took place in Brahmin Boston. What kind of business can the two of us have together? Monkey business! No business! (p. 205)

Kay Campbell, on the other hand, is "hard as a gourd on matters of moral principle, beautifully stubborn in a way I couldn't but envy and adore." Best of all: "*She never raised her voice in an argument.*" Here was not only an intelligent, politically liberal WASP, but one who had "Authority without the temper. Virtue without the self-congratulation. Confidence sans swagger or condescension." Portnoy meets this sturdily built "American" (hence her nickname "The Pumpkin") during his student days at Antioch.

And he who had "never been farther west than Lake Hopatcong in New Jersey" journeys to that "other country" called Davenport, Iowa to spend a weekend with the self-declared "enemy." Unlike the middle-class screamers who populate Roth's *When She Was Good*, the Campbells are Gentiles at their most genteel. Portnoy is both fascinated by the experience ("The English language is *a form of communication!*" he observes, suggesting that things are otherwise in Newark, N. J.) and driven to those special revenges all paranoids imagine:

Please, I pray on the train heading west, let there be no pictures of Jesus Christ in the Campbell house. Let me get through this weekend without having to see his pathetic *punim*—or deal with anyone wearing a cross! When the aunts and uncles come for the Thanksgiving dinner, please, let there be no Anti-Semite among them! Because if someone starts in with 'the pushy Jews,' or says 'kike' or 'jewed him down'—well, I'll jew them down all right. . . . I will shame them and humiliate them in their bigoted hearts! Quote the Declaration of Independence over their candied yams! (p. 223)

Portnoy's worst fears, of course, go unrealized. But, later, Kay misses a period and plans for a suitably "poetic" marriage are romantically dreamed:

We would offer ourselves as resident babysitters to a young faculty couple who were fond of us; in return they would give us their roomy attic to live in, and a shelf to use in their refrigerator. We would wear old clothes and eat spaghetti. . . (p. 229)

And, as Portnoy would have it, we would both be *Jewish*! However, when Kay refuses to convert, the romance crashes on those particular rocks which give the "Temper Tantrum Kid" his identity as the spoiled "nice-Jewish-boy" he actually is.

Finally, there is Sarah Abbot Maulsby, the "Pilgrim." *Her* WASP credentials are even more imposing than the Pumpkin's had been: New Canaan, Foxcroft, Vassar, etc. As a member of the House subcommittee investigation into the television quiz show scandals, Portnoy had gone after people like "Charlatan Van Doren" (the archetypal "ur-WASP") with the vengeance of an Old Testament prophet. Miss Maulsby is thrilled by it all. But, finally, she too is *too, too.* . .

> Why didn't I marry the girl? Well, there was her cutsey-wootsy boarding school argot, for one. Couldn't bear it. 'Barf' for vomit, 'ticked off' for angry, 'a howl' for funny, 'crackers' for crazy, 'teeny' for tiny. . . . Then there were the nicknames of her friends: there were the friends themselves! Poody and Pip and Pebble, Shrimp and Brute and Tug, Squeek, Bumpo, Baba—it sounded, I said, as though she had gone to Vassar with Donald Duck's nephews. (p. 233)

All these abortive relationships can be chalked up easily to the Oedipal complex. But the guilts run even deeper than Portnoy's Independent Study in Freudian theories can explain. *They* are what make the special energy of a culture of sons like Portnoy possible. What he resists, in short, is the fatherhood which is both his destiny and his deepest fear. At one level of consciousness he desperately wants "to grow up to *be* one of these men!"; at another, he is afraid that he, too, will become an avatar of his constipated father.

But in all fairness to the much maligned Jack Portnoy, some of the novel's most poignant moments involve those small gestures of love which Portnoy cannot quite shake off. While a Sophie can be easily pigeon-holed by an insistence that her "biggest fault" is being "too good," Portnoy's father is as complicated as he is long-suffering. It is here that *Portnoy's Complaint* comes closest to the vision of Lawrence's *Sons And Lovers*. To imagine the father "killed," replaced by a younger, more vigorous son is only *part* of the total picture; mothers (who, of course, cannot be "hit") ultimately trouble their sons much more. For all his human weaknesses (at one point Portnoy realizes, sadly, that his father is no

"King Kong" Charlie Keller), Jack Portnoy projects a quiet warmth which may be more important:

> Walks, walks with my father in Weequahic Park on Sundays that I still haven't forgotten. You know, I can't go off to the country and find an acorn on the ground without thinking of him and those walks. And that's not nothing, nearly thirty years later. (p. 94)

Perversion is the result of Portnoy's continuing matrix of attraction/repulsion to all that American–Jewish living seems to imply. In Israel, however, the situation changes as radically as it does "comically." *There* even the bus-drivers and policemen are Jewish; now the ongoing battle between the *goyim* and the Jews no longer makes sense. Here, in short, there are no *schikses*! What Portnoy finds, instead, is Naomi, a militant Israeli as tough in her Marxism as she is confident in her Jewishness. As Portnoy puts it: "a Jewish Pumpkin! *I am being given a second chance.*" We, of course, know better. Impotence—what he will later call "Monkey's Revenge"—is his serio-comic lot.

However, what distinguishes Naomi from the others is her tough-minded assessment of Portnoy's problem. She cuts through his pathetic whining with the sharp edge that Statehood, rather than "exile," presumably provides:

> 'You are the most unhappy person I have ever known. You are like a baby. . . . The way you disapprove of your life! Why do you do that? It is of no value for a man to disapprove of his life the way you do. You seem to take a special pleasure, some pride, in making yourself the butt of your own peculiar sense of humor. I don't believe you actually want to improve your life. Everything you say is somehow always twisted, some way or another, to come out 'funny.' All day long the same thing. In some little way or other, everything is ironical, or self-deprecating.' (p. 264)

Has she, perhaps, hit Portnoy's confessional nail on the head? Perhaps. Roth, on the other hand, knows full well how valuable such built-in criticism can be. It beats *his* commentators to the punch; *he*, after all, is no Portnoy!

But Naomi's words speak to the book's limitations nonetheless. *Portnoy's Complaint* is a minor classic—"minor" in the sense that it chooses to examine a highly selected segment of human experience. Another way of saying the same thing is this: such rambling first-person narratives may be the stuff of a brilliant *tour de force*, but they also have a way of exhausting the possibilities which a "thicker" novel would exploit. In a sense, the novel disappears into the very gags and stand-up comedy which had provided its initial structure.

Indeed, "exhaustion" seems to be the perfect note on which to end a discussion of this novel about psychic exhaustion. For all the zig-zag motion of Portnoy's running "complaint," what he provides is a guide to the "new kvetching" that characterizes the "new steerage":

> .   .   . I am not in this boat alone, oh no, I am on the biggest troop
> ship afloat.   .   . only look in through the portholes and see us there,
> stacked to the bulkheads in our bunks, moaning and groaning with
> such pity for ourselves, the sad and watery-eyed sons of Jewish parents,
> sick to the gills from rolling through these heavy seas of guilt—so I
> sometimes envision us, me and my fellow wailers, melancholics, and
> wise guys, still in steerage, like our forebears—and sick, sick as dogs,
> we cry out intermittently, one of us or the other, 'Poppa, how could
> you? 'Momma, why did you?' and the stories we tell, as the big ship
> pitches and rolls, the vying we do—who had the most castrating mother,
> who the most benighted father, I can match you, you bastard, humilia-
> tion, shame for shame.   .   .   . (pp. 117-118)

Portnoy's Complaint is obviously the big winner in such a contest. It is a book that had to be done as much as it is the book Roth had to do. As Portnoy bravely tears off the "Do Not Remove Under Penalty of Law" tag from his matress and prepares to die with the bravado of a Humphrey Bogart ("while I lived, *I lived big*!"), the self-destructive monologue comes to an end—and his analyst can, at long last, begin. Circular and systematically non-conclusive, *Portnoy's Complaint* laid out all the psychic pieces in a rush of comically verbal pyrotechnics. More importantly, it was the culmination of an urban, American-Jewish idiom which remains Roth's most congenial literary turf. It will survive—yes, even one day transcend—the assorted noise which has surrounded it. Because, for better or worse, with this book Roth provides both a chronicle and an epitaph for those times, that place.

Notes

1   Leslie Fiedler, *Waiting for the End* (New York: Stein and Day, 1964), pp. 67-68. Subsequent references to Professor Fiedler are to the chapter of this book entitled "Zion as Main Street" and pagination is given parenthetically.

2   Robert Alter, *After the Tradition* (New York: E. P. Dutton & Co., 1969), p. 117.

3   Philip Roth, *Goodbye, Columbus* (Boston: Houghton Mifflin, 1967), p. 6. Subsequent references to *Goodbye, Columbus* are to this edition and pagination is given parenthetically.

4   Philip Roth, *Portnoy's Complaint* (New York: Random House, 1969), pp. 93-94. Subsequent references to *Portnoy's Complaint* are to this edition and pagination is given parenthetically.

5   Melvin Friedman, "Jewish Mothers and Sons: The expense of Chutzpah," in Irving Malin, ed. *Contemporary American—Jewish Literature: Critical Essays* (Bloomington: Indiana University Press, 1973), p. 170.

6   Norman Podhoretz, *Making It* (New York: Random House, 1967), *passim*.

7   Irving Howe, "Philip Roth Reconsidered," *Commentary*, LIV, No. 6 (December 1972), 76.

IV

Christ as Revolutionary/Revolutionary as Christ:
The Hero in Bernard Malamud's THE FIXER and
William Styron's THE CONFESSIONS OF NAT TURNER

> *"To represent and illustrate the past, the*
> *actions of men, is the task of either writer*
> *[i.e. historian and novelist] and the only*
> *difference that I can see is, in proportion as*
> *he succeeds, to the honor of the novelist."*
>
> —*Henry James*

The writing of novels and the writing of history share much,
not the least of which is the highly conscious art of selection. History has always been more than the endless compilation of "facts"
in much the same way that novels are more than a series of unedit-
ed tape recordings. From a myriad of information, each man must
choose which events will be highlighted, which suppressed, which
made to seem of crucial importance and which merely trivial. It is
the *shaping*, then, of both novels and history which gives a uniquely
private dimension to what may, at first glance, look to be totally
public property.

James spoke with a deadly seriousness when he claimed that
"the novel *is* history"—and his assessment of Trollope suggests why
he thought so:

I was lately struck, in reading over many pages of Anthony Trollope,
with his want of discretion in this particular. In a digression, a paren-
thesis or an aside, he concedes to the reader that he and this trusting
friend are only "making believe." He admits that the events he narrates
have not really happened, and that he can give his narrative any turn
the reader may like best. Such a betrayal of a sacred office seems to
me, I confess, a terrible crime; it is what I mean by the attitude of
apology, and it shocks me every whit as much in Trollope as it would
have shocked me in Gibbon or Macaulay. It implies that the novelist is

less occupied in looking for the truth (the truth, of course I mean, that he assumes, the premises that we must grant him, whatever they may be) than the historian, and in doing so it deprives him at a stroke of all his standing room.[1] (pp. 390-391)

But eloquent claims for overlap aside, there are some striking differences in both the assumptions and the ways that historians and novelists actually work. Novelists are far more likely to draw their sustenance from those mythic patterns which have existed since primordial time and which still can speak to the deepest levels of man's consciousness. To plumb the *essence* of an event is to establish a connection between the specific and the universal, between an individual man and the total human condition. For the novelist, linkage is made by an act of the imagination, but the fiction which results may tell us truths about history that no amount of research in the archives of "fact" can equal.

In the 1960's, however, the mythic dimensions a William Faulkner had staked out as the "sole owner and proprietor" of Yoknapatapha County or an Ernest Hemingway fished for along the Big Two-Hearted River were replaced by the growing appeal of *actual* history. What Tom Wolfe has called the "new journalism"— *reportage* that subjects the immediate and "real" to the metaphorical fireworks usually associated with first-rate fiction—threatens to make the Faulkners and Hemingways seem terribly old-fashioned. There is no question, I think, that journalism's gain of a Truman Capote or a Norman Mailer has been literature's loss. However, what Styron calls a "meditation on history" or what Capote and Mailer have done in the development of the non-fictional novel has created an important sub-genre, one which speaks to the human heart with all the mythic power that had once been the province of fiction alone.

To be sure, this merging of history and literature has not come without a certain amount of loss. For Faulkner, the writer's business was to look into what he called "the human heart in conflict with itself," and to report, with as much honesty as possible, about the findings. This, I submit, is never an easy matter, and literature is filled with examples of faulty imaginations, imperfect shapings, failed visions. However, if the "human Heart" in question happens to belong to Nat Turner, black leader of a slave revolt during the 1830's and his author happens to be a very white Southerner named William Styron, responses to the work are likely to be depressingly predictable and usually always extra-literary.

It might be well at this point, to recall one last bit of advice from Mr. James:

> We must grant the artist his subject, his ideas, his donnée; our criticism is applied only to what he makes of it.

The stories of Mendele Beiliss and Nat Turner were rich in historical context, but richer still in fictive possibilities. If James is right, though, the *real* question is how and what the respective authors made of these men and *that* is the question with which I shall attempt to deal.

The ironies of the publishing industry are sometimes as interesting as the ironies they publish. In 1966 two books appeared (almost simultaneously) dealing with the all-but-forgotten trial of Mendele Beiliss. The first was Maurice Samuel's *Blood Accusation*, a heavily documented, yet eminently readable, account of the events surrounding Beiliss's trial. Mr. Samuel came to his work with all the energy and skill of the professional researcher—relying on transcripts of the actual proceedings and an impressive bibliography of works dealing with the Russian temper at the turn of the century. The trial itself had stirred a considerable amount of international attention in 1911, but was seemingly swallowed up in the rush of events following the Revolution and World War I. In fact, it *never* had the sort of glamor and spectacular foreign intrigue associated with the Dreyfus case, nor was it enshrined by the prose of Emile Zola or the acting of Paul Muni. Prior to Samuel's study, only one full-length book about the trial had been published (Alexander Tager's *The Decay Of Czarism: The Beiliss Trial* in 1935) and *it* had been widely ignored.

Bernard Malamud, on the other hand, came to the Beiliss story with more of an eye on its mythic possibilities than its historical dimensions. Samuel tells us that Mendele Beiliss was thirty-nine at the time of his trial, the father of five children and a rather nondescript person on the whole. He was known to his friends as *nash* Mendel—our Mendel—and as Samuel points out:

> The role that the prosecution tried to thrust on Beiliss, that of the

fanatical killer of Christian children and drinker of their blood, had something ludicrous about it in the midst of its obscenity. Had it at last been some picturesque and exotic figure, some beetle-browed, white-bearded *exalte*—but *nash* Mendel! Nor was he cut out for the role in which others tried to cast him, that of the hero and unflinching martyr. . . . He did not want to be in history; he wanted to be left alone.[2] (pp. 59-60)

In Malamud's novel *The Fixer*, Beiliss becomes Yakov Bok, a name rich with the sort of ambiguities Malamud envisioned for his protagonist. In Yiddish, "bok" means "goat" with all the implications of stubbornness that it implies. However, "bok" might also be a pun on the English word "balk." And, finally, there are strong hints throughout the novel that the protagonist's name is an anagram for "Bog," the Russian word for God. In a novel as consciously crafted as *The Fixer*, Malamud has changed Beiliss's name with more in mind than merely a protection of the innocent.

For the *real* Mendele Beiliss, the blood accusation meant a long year's wait in jail and a trial so absurd it might have been a comic opera by Gilbert and Sullivan. When he was finally acquitted friends helped him emigrate to Palestine. In 1922 Beiliss moved to the United States, trying his hand at printing and, later, at selling insurance. He had as little success in America as he had had in Palestine, although he did manage to sell the story of his trial to a Yiddish newspaper in 1925. By the time of his death in 1934 both Mendele Beiliss and the most infamous blood libel trial of the twentieth century had slipped into obscurity.

Malamud's Yakov Bok, on the other hand, moves through *his* encounter with history as if it were an archetypal journey of learning. Emotionally speaking, Yakov begins the novel at ground zero. The shtetl in which he is forced to live—like the grocery stores one finds in a Malamud novel like *The Assistant*—is a tomb, a place where "opportunity is born dead." His own father

had been killed in an incident not more than a year after Yakov's birth—something less than a pogrom, and less than useless: two drunken soldiers shot the first three Jews in their path, his father had been the second.[3] (p. 4)

And, as if this were not enough, his wife, Raisl, deserts him after seven years of a childless marriage. Yakov responds to his collective misfortunes by combining a highly developed skepticism with lingering hopes for an inner life.

Significantly enough, Yakov begins his journey into the world beyond the shtetl at the age of thirty. However, like the bumbling college professor of Malamud's *A New Life*, Yakov finds the road much harder than he had imagined. He offers a ride to an old woman, only to have his wagon break down almost immediately. Even

> with hatchet, saw, plane, tin-smith's shears, tri-square, putty, wire, pointed knife and two awls, the fixer couldn't fix what was broken. (p. 22)

In many respects the scene is a synecdoche for much of Yakov's trouble throughout the novel. As the "fixer," Yakov has faith in his tools and in his ability to use them—even though the *facts* of his ill-fated experiences would seem to indicate otherwise.

When Yakov arrives finally in Kiev, he "went looking for luck"—only to find, instead, a drunken Russian lying in the snow. The man is wearing the emblem of the Black Hundreds (an anti-Semitic organization roughly equivalent to our Ku Klux Klan) and, although Bok is "afraid to be involved in trouble," he rescues him nonetheless. What follows is an ironic parody of the Joseph story: Yakov, very much the alien in a foreign land, rises to the position of overseer in the anti-Semite's brick factory. He moves into a restricted neighborhood, keeps his Jewishness a secret, and goes about the risky business of assimilation.

The part of Potiphar's wife is played by the crippled daughter of Yakov's boss, complete with noctural temptations and guilt-ridden refusals. Eventually Yakov, like Joseph, is falsely accused (one of the charges being "attempted rape") and thrown into a dungeon where his Joseph-like dreams take on a distinctly Dostoievskian character.

An important barometer of Yakov's development is his growing involvement with mankind and his eventual commitment to the political process. When he first arrived at Kiev, Yakov was neither a maker of waves nor a receiver of wooden nickels—particularly where partisan politics were concerned. As he put it in those pristine and undisturbed days:

> I am not a political person. The world's full of it but it's not for me. Politics is not my nature. (p. 45)

However, when Yakov is accused of ritual murder and the State methodically cranks out the Big Lie, Yakov's "nature" begins to change. From utter bewilderment and disbelief ("The fixer readily confessed he was a Jew. Otherwise he was innocent"), Yakov came to envision "terrible things happening to him, ending by being torn apart by a mob."

In a very real sense Yakov only begins his figurative journey of learning when all possibilities of literal movement have ended. During the early stages of his imprisonment, Yakov sustains himself by recalling the epigrams of Ibn Ezra, sentiments which have their place in the luckless history of former schlemiels:

> He feared the prison would go badly for him and it went badly at once. It's my luck, he thought bitterly. What do they [i.e. Ibn Ezra] say?— 'If I dealt in candles the sun wouldn't set.' Instead, I'm Yakov Fixer and it sets each hour on the stroke. I'm the kind of man who finds it perilous to be alive. One thing I must learn is to say less—much less, or I'll ruin myself. As it is I'm already ruined. (p. 143)

But as Yakov's years in prison begin to parallel Christ's last years on earth, their mutual suffering makes for strong points of identification. Given a copy of the New Testament, Yakov read the story of the

> strange Jew, humorless and fanatic, but the fixer liked the teachings and read with pleasure of the healing of the lame, blind and of the epileptics who fell into fire and water. He enjoyed the loaves and fishes and the raising of the dead. In the end he was deeply moved when he read how they spat on him and beat him with sticks; and he hung on the cross at night. (p. 232)

Yakov's lawyer tells him that, like Christ, "You suffer for us all" and in one of Yakov's most striking dreams he imagines that the murdered child

> came to him with his punctured face and bleeding chest and begged for the return of his life. Yakov laid both hands on the boy and tried to raise him from the dead but it wouldn't work. (p. 319)

And, yet, Yakov's increasing involvement with humanity is more a matter of reconstituting his own humanity than any sustained drive toward becoming a symbolic Christ. For example, he acknowledged Raisl's illegitimate son as his own (the boy, significantly enough, is named Chaim or "life") and finds himself capable of felt emotion at the deaths of Bibikov and Shmuel. All this despite the fact that Yakov claims "what suffering has taught me is the uselessness of suffering. . ."

Gone, too, are Yakov's illusions about the possibilities of living outside the stream of history. As he puts it:

> Once you leave, you're out in the open; it rains and snows. It snows history, which means what happens to somebody starts in a web of events outside the personal. It starts of course before he gets there. We're all in history, that's sure, but some are more than others. Jews more than some. . . . Nobody lived in Eden any more. . . . Why? Because no Jew was innocent in a corrupt state, the most visible sign of its corruption its fear and hatred of those it persecuted. (pp. 314-315)

The Fixer's final learning is a manifesto for revolution. When the Tsar (appearing before Yakov in the last of his tortured fantasies) suggests that *he* is really the "victim, the sufferer for my poor people," Yakov shoots without hesitation:

> As for history, there are ways to reverse it. What the Tsar deserves is a bullet in the gut. Better him than us. (p. 334)

Malamud leaves the outcome of the Fixer's trial open-ended, purposefully ambiguous. The novel itself ends as Yakov (now thirty-three) is being driven to the courthouse through streets already erupting into violence. His final words, however, leave no doubt about what the prison experience has taught him and what he would do in the event he were freed:

> One thing I've learned, he thought, there's no such thing as an unpolitical man, especially a Jew. You can't be one without the other, that's clear enough. You can't sit still and see yourself destroyed. . . . If the state acts in ways that are abhorrent to human nature it's the lesser evil to destroy it. Death to the anti-Semites! Long live revolution! Long live liberty! (p. 335)

Malamud's novel works hard to convince us that the Mendele

Beiliss we remembered as a scapegoat of history was really a fire-breathing revolutionary all along. William Styron's *The Confessions Of Nat Turner* is out to do much the same thing, only this time in the opposite direction. Ours is an age which has become highly sensitized to what the paperback anthologists like to call "black rage" and, therefore, it should come as no great surprise that while Bernard Malamud's fictional portrait of Mendele Beiliss went largely unchallenged, William Styron's Nat Turner did not. *The Fixer* is, of course, more solidly in the tradition of fiction and thus more likely to reap the benefits of a reader's willing suspension of disbelief. *The Confessions.*   . ., on the other hand, is out for *kudos* on three nearly equal fronts—as novel, as history, and as a "meditation on history"—in a triangle of genres with such equilateral sides that liabilities on one end can be balanced by assets on the other two. Or, at least, this seems to be Styron's hope; it is one shared by those who labor in this vineyard of built-in victories called the "new journalism."

As a work of historical scholarship *The Confessions Of Nat Turner* has generated more controversy than any book published in the last decade, with the possible exception of the *Warren Commission Report*. Styron's claim that he "rarely departed from the *known* facts about Nat Turner and the revolt of which he was the leader" hit highly sensitive nerves and opened a can of worms which continue to crawl through the pages of public print. Herbert Aptheker, author of the highly regarded study *American Negro Slave Revolts* (1943) attacked Styron's irresponsible scholarship and deliberate manipulation of fact in magazines like *Political Affairs* and *The Nation*. He pointed out that the Nat Turner incident was *not*, as Styron so blithely claimed, "the only effective, sustained revolt in the annals of American Negro slavery"—that, as a matter of *real* fact, such uprisings had been occurring in Virginia on a fairly regular basis since 1691. To be sure, one can always speculate about the number of people who have to "rise" before there is a legitimate *uprising*, but that is rather like asking how many swallows make a summer.

Black writers were particularly anxious to set the record straight. In a collection of essays entitled *Ten Black Writers Respond* (John Henry Clarke, ed.) they accused Styron, in page after tedious page, of "stealing their Nat." A few of the charges deal directly with matters of historical accuracy, such as the deliberate suppression of the facts about Nat Turner's family life included in the acknowledged source of Styron's book (Thomas Gray's "Confessions of Nat Turner," 1831).

But for all the talk about Styron's mismanagement of historical facts, the contributors of *Ten Black Writers Respond* were not so much out to question his "scholarship" as they were to expose him as a white racist who had no damn business writing such a novel in the first place. As one of the writers—Alvin Poussaint—put it:

> In the author's note.   . . Styron refers to Nat Turner as 'Nat.' Is this familiarity by the author part of his intuitive white condescension and adherance to southern racial etiquette? Is this reference and the entire book an unconscious attempt to keep Nat Turner 'in his place'—to emasculate him? Would the novelist expect Nat Turner to address him as 'Mr. Styron'?[4]

To anyone with first-hand experience in the psychodynamics of the black/white confrontation, rhetoric of this sort must have a depressingly familiar ring. Obviously, a copy of *Understanding Fiction* and a crash course in the Contemporary Novel will not do; the black psyche, we are told, is so unique that it can only respond to *black* literature written by *black* authors and taught by *black* professors. The situation is further complicated by the fact that one's "blackness" is directly related to one's level of overt militancy, thereby disenfranchising any "Toms" who might disagree in advance. Mr. Jervis Anderson, a black writer himself, has written an eminently sensible reply to this position in the March-April, 1969, issue of *Dissent*, part of which I shall quote at some length:

> But since one of the impressions gained by the black critics is that Styron, as a white man, labored under a fatal difficulty in his attempt to portray a black Turner, it might be useful to pause here and consider some of the implications of this controversy for black writers defining their own historical situation. On the basis of precedent alone—the excellent portrayal of Negro character by Faulkner and Gertrude Stein, to name only two—it seems rather absurd to suggest that white American novelists are incapable of perceiving and portraying black character. And it becomes even more absurd when one considers that no black American writer has even been heard to speak of the impossibility or the impertinence of blacks portraying white character. To make such a claim, then, is almost to suggest that the imagination as the crucial instrument of artistic creation enjoys a free and vigorous life

among black writers but is moribund and impotent among those who are white.

> Actually, if that is what the claim of the black writers insists, it is much too absurd to stand for what they really mean. What they must really mean is that the imagination should be suborned into relating not what it sees but what is politically or sociologically expedient to be seen. And looked at in those terms, it becomes clear that a part of the critical animus against Styron resides in his critic's demand that literature should serve the immediate ideological interests of the black community—in the same way that the Communist critics of the thirties demanded that literature should consciously serve the aims and objectives of the class struggle.[5] (p. 161)

Despite all the claims and counter-claims about the historical accuracy of Styron's Nat Turner, the truth is we know precious little about him. There is, of course, Thomas Gray's original "Confessions," but they are more than suspect and the same is true of William Drewry's *The Southamption Insurrection* (1900). Herbert Aptheker has published a slim volume entitled *Nat Turner's Slave Rebellion* (1966), but it is more valuable as a study of the socioeconomic conditions which gave rise to the incident than as a biography of its leader. For better or worse, then, Nat Turner was *already* a shadowy figure when Styron began his book. All the present bickering is really a matter of deciding what dimensions his "fictional" outline ought to take.

Styron's Nat Turner is, it seems to me, a richly ambivalent character whose internal tensions are most often reflected in the metaphorical structures of his various languages. Jervis Anderson is dead right when he suggests that

> this is not to say the elaborately stylized language Styron employs comes anywhere close to reflecting the consciousness of a black slave rebel of 1831. If anything, it strains away from credibility rather than toward it. (p. 159)

And, yet, if by some magic a writer *could* reproduce the actual speech of a black slave rebel of 1831, the results would not only be unreadable, they would be fictionally uninteresting. After all, *nobody* ever talked like Holden Caulfield nor do the Molly Blooms of the world dream in such ordered streams-of-consciousness. Writers give us the *illusions* of speech, not the actual speech itself. Nat's highly conscious manipulation of "nigger talk" ("Just a little bitty piece of pone. . . . Please, young mastah. I'm dreadful hungry") is played against the eloquence of his interior monologues in much the same way that Old Testament wrath is pitted against the language of New Testament redemption. The language of Nat's sermons is a curious blend of "nigger talk" (used with full knowledge of its potential for condescension) and the current rhetoric about black pride we have been hearing from people like Stokely Carmichael:

> But oh, my brothers, black folks ain't never goin' to be led from bondage without they has *pride*! Black folk ain't goin' to be free, they ain't goin' to have no spoonbread an' sweet cider less'n they studies to love they own *selves*. Only then will the first be last, and the last first. Black folk ain't never goin' to be no great nation until they studies to love their own black skin an' the beauty of that skin an' the beauty of them hands. . . . Pride! I cried after a pause, and let my arms descend. 'Pride, pride, everlasting pride, pride will make you free!'[6]

Styron seems to accept Thomas Gray's portrait of Nat Turner as religious fanatic in ways which tend to emasculate the history and most certainly the politics of the revolt, but *not*, I would submit, Nat Turner himself. The substance of Styron's Nat Turner lies in his religious fantasies, in his drive toward a prophetic mission which is always counterpointed by his capacity for Christ-like love. When Nat's black pride speech concluded,

> Others drew toward me [i.e. Nat Turner], radiant; and Henry, who was deaf, who had read my lips, came up close to me and silently clasped my arm. I heard Nelson say, 'You done spoke de truth,' and he too drew near, and I felt their warmth and brotherhood and hope and knew then what Jesus must have known when upon the shores of Galilee he said: '*Follow me, and I will make you fishers of men.*' (p. 298)

And, yet, Nat is *not* his followers. There is more at stake here than the separation between "house" and "field" niggers or even that Nat is the most educated slave in Southampton County. Nat is a man with a vision, a creator of black myth and somewhat of a black god figure himself. But such leadership is a lonely business and it is not long before Nat *becomes* what he hates:

> . . . I told them about Napoleon Bonaparte. . . who was transformed by me, with the utmost guile, into a seven-foot black prodigy and the scourge of all white creation. Lord, how I strove to drive the idea of a nigger Napoleon into their savage minds! Naturally, I wished

to implant there too a sense of black militancy and I was gratified to see how through my clever guidance they were able to identify with this murderous conqueror. Like Joshua and David (turned also into Negro heroes by my artful tongue) he bestrode the wreckage of the white man's world like an angel of the apocalypse. I described him as an African risen to sweep up and annihilate the white tribes of the North. However, childishly, they came to believe in this dark demigod; their eyes glittered when I told them of his conquests, and it seemed to me I saw deep in those eyes the sparks of a new-born courage—hints, auguries of a passion for blood that needed only my final prick of animation to explode into fury. I forbore, however, trying to teach these more simple and benighted of my followers to read or count. In their twenties or thirties, most of them, they were too old for such frills, besides, what good would it do in the end? Not of course did I yet intimate by the vaguest sign or word the true nature of my great plans. It was enough now, as the time grew short, that they stand in awe of me and warm to the light I knew I shed of inelectable wisdom and power. (pp. 316-317)

One could see this passage as clear evidence that Nat is nothing more than a Massah-in-blackface who treats his followers like "chillen" and fully intends to keep them that way. Or it may be that this is simply the stuff of leadership, the way rebellions of any color are made. Masters, inevitably, become contemptuous of their disciples.

At the same time, however, the nature of Nat's rhetoric keeps pulling us back to the religious fanaticism which lies at the very core of his motivations. The bloody march to Jerusalem begins, more and more, to sound like Armageddon and one is never quite sure if it will be Christ, Moses, a black Napoleon or God himself who will be leading the conquering army. At one point in the novel Judge Cobb describes Virginia as

A wasteland! A plump and virginal principality, a cornucopia of riches the like of which the world has never seen, transformed within the space of a century to a withering, defeated hag! (p. 77)

In a very real sense, it is Nat who envisions himself as the myth-opoeic Hero who can regenerate the barren land and lift the curse of slavery from his people.

To be sure, the purity required for such a mission makes some heavy demands on the human psyche. Nat's sexual vacillaations, for example, are a kind of shorthand way of representing the tension between Nat's commitment to the spiritual and his growing attraction to the fleshly. The situation is further complicated by Nat's reluctance and/or inability to express love in anything but sexual terms. For much of the novel his sexual experiences are almost entirely voyeuristic. He *sees* the white man fornicate and unconsciously associates a growing hatred of whites with his own compulsive drives toward chastity. His homosexual encounter with Willis works in nearly the same way. Nat translates his "hungry tenderness" into a physical experience and then feels guilt because it has separated him from God:

> . . . I knew I must consecrate myself to the Lord's service from this point on, as I had promised Him, avoiding at all costs such pleasures of the flesh as I had experienced that morning. If I could be shaken to my very feet by this unsought-for encounter with a boy, think what it might be, I reflected, think what an obstacle would be set in my path toward spiritual perfection if I should have any commerce with a *woman*! (p. 203)

When Willis is conveniently sold down the river—thus resolving Nat's sexual dilemma—the incident becomes one more reason to hasten the day of revolution.

But the thought of "commerce with a *woman*!" continues to plague Nat at the deepest levels of his consciousness. Ultimately the grotesquely foolish Margaret Whitehead must be destroyed if Nat's Old Testament vengeance is to triumph over his more Christ-like inclinations. Jervis Anderson suggests that:

> It is this religious mania that seems responsible for his sexual continence and frustration; it is a combination of the mania and frustration that seems to account for his impulse to rebellion; it is a conflict between Old and New Testament commands that leads him to falter over his only act of killing; and it is also this conflict that seems responsible for the sense of ambivalence and even regret with which he assesses his role in the rebellion. (p. 164)

The Confessions Of Nat Turner opens with Nat in his cell, his rebellion betrayed and crushed. As Gray is quick to point out, it was "*them other niggers, dragooned, balked, it was them other niggers that cooked your goose, Reverend!*" A cock crows, then another, and finally Nat hears a horn blow softly out of Jerusalem.

A bit heavy-handed perhaps, but Styron is out to shift Nat from a wild-eyed, Old Testament prophet to an avatar of Christ. The rebellion is over. Nat now has doubts about the authenticity of the "voices" he heard. The atmosphere is the sort one might find in Kierkegaard's *Fear And Trembling* and, as a matter of fact, there are striking parallels between the two works. In addition, Gray gives a thumbnail sketch of the twentieth century's fascination with the death of God which must have sounded rather strange in 1831:

> *Christianity*! Rapine, plunder, butchery! Death and destruction! And misery and suffering for untold generations. That was the accomplishment of your Christianity, Reverend. That was the fruits of your mission. And that was the joyous message of your faith. Nineteen hundred years of Christian teaching plus a black preacher is all it takes—is all it takes to prove that God is a God darned lie! (p. 118)

The first section of the novel (significantly entitled "Judgment Day") ends with Nat bewildered, visibly shaken and wondering if

> maybe he [i.e. Gray] is right.   .   . maybe all was for nothing, maybe worse than nothing, and all I've done was evil in the sight of God. Maybe he is right and God is dead and gone, which is why I can no longer reach him.   .   . *Then what I done was wrong Lord.   .   . And if what I done was wrong, is there no redemption?*
>
> I raised my eyes upward but there was no answer, only the gray impermeable sky and night falling fast over Jerusalem. (p. 120)

The answer to Nat's question comes on the book's final page, thus completing a framework through which we can see the meaning of Nat Turner and his ill-fated rebellion. The answer, of course, is *love* and it comes in a vision of Margaret's voice as Nat is led off to his death:

> *We'll love one another*, she seems to be entreating me, very close now, *we'll love one another by the light of heaven above.* I feel the nearness of flowing water, tumultuous waves, rushing winds. The voice calls again: 'Come.' (pp. 403-404)

And so Nat dies: Christ-like and martyred, he speeds off to rewards on the other side of the grave. In the final analysis, *The Confessions Of Nat Turner* is a brave, yet foolish book. At times all the sexual/

religious trauma make it sound like a Black Baptist version of *St. Augustine's Confessions*. Furthermore, Malamud's "fiction" makes for fewer built-in problems than Styron's "history"—particularly when it is Nat's psyche (not his history) which is Styron's *real* interest. And, finally, Styron's mythmaking would have been easier—and, I suspect, more effective—if he had not tied himself to the words of Thomas Gray's "Confessions" and his own words in the "Author's Note." In the 1960's, however, "history" had a magic that was as fatal as it was falsified. One thing is clear though: Styron did not *steal* anybody's Nat—he simply created his own. After Maurice Samuel's *Blood Accusation* and Bernard Malamud's *The Fixer*, chances are good that we will see neither Mendele Beiliss nor his fictional counterparts next Passover. But with Nat Turner. . . ah, *that* is another matter, one which has not been satisfactorily resolved in "history" or in the stuff we continue to call *fiction*.

Notes

1   Henry James, "The Art of Fiction" in Morton D. Zabel, ed., *The Portable Henry James* (New York: Viking, 1951), pp. 390-391.

2   Maurice Samuel, *Blood Accusation* (New York: Alfred A. Knopf, 1966), pp. 59-60.

3.   Bernard Malamud, *The Fixer* (New York: Farrar, Straus and Giroux, 1966), p. 4. Subsequent references to *The Fixer* are to this edition and pagination is given parenthetically.

4.   Alvin Poussaint, "*The Confessions of Nat Turner* and the Dilemma of William Styron," in John Henrik Clarke, ed., *William Styron's Nat Turner: Ten Black Writers Respond* (Boston: Beacon Press, 1968), p. 117.

5   Jervis Anderson, "Styron and His Black Critics," *Dissent* (March-April 1969), p. 161.

6   William Styron, *The Confessions Of Nat Turner* (New York: Signet edition, 1968), pp. 297-298. Subsequent references to *The Confessions Of Nat Turner* are to this edition and pagination is given parenthetically.

V

John Barth: The Teller Who Swallowed His Tale

Avant-garde writing tends to be an "ify" thing these days, more a matter of cocktail chatter than execution. The resources for experiments worth the doing seem used up or, as John Barth himself once put it, "exhausted."[1]   This is not an especially *new* predicament for the would-be writer, but it is one which looms larger in an age of self-conscious, anxious Art. Looking backward may reduce the novelist to an imitative pillar of salt, his novel to mere carbon copy. On the other hand, pop art dangles in the horizon, promising to make good on any manifesto which begins "What if I?.   .   . (a) break out of linear print altogether (b) replace order with chapters that can be re-shuffled to suit each reader (c) write the whole damn thing on a roll of toilet paper.

Since his impressive debut with *The Floating Opera* (1956), John Barth has lived somewhere in the crunch between. The highly reflexive inward motion of his narrative energy extends the mood of innovators like Gide and Proust at the same time that it transposes the agony of sheer storytelling into new, and often exciting keys. Reflexivity, after all, was a logical outgrowth of Modernism's solipsistic tendencies, a way of creating artistic worlds-within-worlds and equating the creative act with the artistic product. Marcel Proust's *Remembrance Of Things Past* is obsessed with its own creation; in André Gide's *The Counterfiters*, a novelist keeps a diary about a novelist keeping a diary. And in *Point Counterpoint* the technique reaches that reduction to absurdity Huxley could never quite resist. His persona—a disillusioned, all too cerebral writer—muses about the possibility of putting a "novelist into the novel." And then he wonders: "Why not a second inside his? And a third inside the novel of the second?" Etc. Etc.

Translated in Barthian terminology, the result is "imitation" of a very special sort; indeed, he may be the most poetically self-conscious novelist of them all:

> Whether historically the novel expires or persists seems immaterial to
> me; if enough writers and critics *feel* apocalyptical about it, their
> feeling becomes a considerable cultural fact, like the *feeling* that
> Western civilization, or the world, is going to end rather soon. . . . If
> you happened to be Vladimir Nabokov, you might address that felt
> urgency by writing *Pale Fire*: a fine novel by a learned pedant, in the
> form of a pedantic commentary on a poem invented for the purpose.
> If you were a Borges, you might write *Labyrinths*: fictions by a learned
> librarian in the form of footnotes, as he describes them, to imaginary
> or hypothetical books. And I'll add, since I believe Borges' idea is
> rather interesting, that if you were the author of this paper, you'd have
> written something like *Sot-Weed Factor* or *Giles Goat-Boy*: novels
> which imitate the form of the Novel, by an author who imitates the
> role of Author. 2

Barth's strongest suit has always been parody, a double-edged
form which simultaneously pays tribute to its models and under-
mines them. *Sot-Weed Factor* (1965) and *Giles Goat-Boy* (1967) are
the most obvious examples, if only because their extended length
allows Barth to build worlds (eighteenth century America, in one
case; an allegorical Academy in the other), rather than the isolated
islands of, say, *Lost In The Funhouse* (1968) or his recent *Chimera*
(1973). But parody, even in hindsight, is nearly as slippery a business as a Barthian character. The atmosphere which pervades *The
Floating Opera* (1956) floats throughout the canon. Todd Andrews
(an existentially comic narrator who might have been at home in
Ford Madox Ford's *The Good Soldier*)3 cannot quite remember the
date of his story. On either June 23rd or 24th, 1937, he decided,
finally, not to kill himself. Ambivalence—albeit of a comic rather
than New Critical sort—is his leitmotif; wacky rationalism is his
method. Even his *name* contributes to the hyper-serious good
cheer:

> So. Yes, my name. Todd Andrews is my name. You can spell it with
> one or two *d*'s. I get letters addressed either way. I almost warned you
> against the single-*d* spelling, for fear you'd say, '*Tod* is German for
> death; perhaps the name is symbolic.' I myself use two *d*'s, partly in
> order to avoid that symbolism. But you see, I ended by not warning
> you at all, and that's because it just occurred to me that the double-*d*
> *Todd* is symbolic, too, and accurately so. *Tod* is death, and this book
> hasn't much to do with death; *Todd* is almost Tod—that is, almost
> death—and this book, if it gets written, has very much to do with
> almost death.4

An intruding narrator, to be sure, but one out to warn deep, Modernist readers to beware. At another point Andrews offers up a wartime memory filled with the stuff that makes Freudian critics drool—only to wryly stand back, change gears and catch the overly analytical off-guard:

> Now you must read this paragraph with an open mind: I can't warn you too often not to make the quickest, easiest judgments of me, if you're interested in being accurate. The next thing I did was lay aside my rifle, bayonet and all, lie in the mud beside this animal [i.e. the German sergeant] whom I'd reduced to paralysis, and embrace him as fiercely as any man ever embraced his mistress. I covered his dirty stubbled face with kisses: his staring eyes, his lolling tongue, his shuddering neck. Incredibly, now that I look back on it, he responded in kind! The fear had left him, as it had left me, and for an hour, I'm sure, we clung to each other frenziedly. We were one man.
>
> If the notion of homosexuality enters your head, you're normal, I think. If you judge either the German sergeant or myself to have been homosexual, you're stupid. (p. 73)

Unfortunately, gamsy narrators have a nasty habit of overplaying their hands. Believe what they say on page one: "I was born in San Francisco, so it is hardly a surprise that summers seemed like winters to me" and you will come in for a shot of cheap scorn two chapters later: "Dear reader, forget about San Francisco and all that stuff about non-existent summers. Actually, my birthplace was Kearny, Nebraska, where the winds blow cold as the proverbial witch's teat." Barth, however, has always been at the controls of his comic "operas," no matter how much they seem to "float" at first glance. If nothing else, the mushrooming academic criticism about his work suggests (ironically enough, I suppose) that there is structure and technique a'plenty. But the canon itself provides all the necessary clues, particularly if one takes the following passage as a kind of reading guide for the work to come:

> It always seemed a fine idea to me to build a showboat with just one big flat open deck on it, and to keep a play going continuously. The boat wouldn't be moored, but would drift up and down the river on the tide, and the audience would sit along both banks. They would catch whatever part of the plot happened to unfold as the boat floated past, and then they'd have to wait until the tide ran back again to catch another snatch of it, if they still happened to be sitting there. To fill in the gaps they'd have to use their imaginations, or ask more attentive

neighbors, or hear the word passed along from upriver or downriver.
most times they wouldn't understand what was going on at all, or
they'd think they knew, when actually they didn't. Lots of times
they'd be able to see the actors, but not hear them. Need I explain?
That's how so much of life works: our friends float past; we become
involved with them; they float on, and we must rely on hearsay or
lose track of them completely; they float back again, and we must
either renew our friendship—catch up to date—or find that they and
we don't comprehend each other any more. And that's how this book
[i.e. *The Floating Opera*] will work, I'm sure. It's a floating opera,
friend, chock-full of curiosities, melodrama, spectacle, instruction
and entertainment, but it floats willy-nilly on the tide of my vagrant
prose: you'll catch sight of it, then lose it, then spy it again; and it will
doubtless require the best effort of your attention and imagination—
together with no little patience, if you're an average fellow—to keep
track of the plot as it sails in and out of view. (pp. 13-14)

Lost In The Funhouse makes good on such reflexive promises. This time, however, the art of storytelling threatens to become
the whole story. All the standard Barthian themes are there: marital
triangles, unbridled flux, chameleonesque characters and the rest.
It is, in short, the stuff that had provided the comic energy of *Sot-
Weed Factor* and *Giles Goat-Boy*. But, by now, one began to have
the eerie feeling that Barth himself was getting stuck on the mobius
strip which provides the collection with its "Frame Tale":

> ONCE UPON A TIME THERE WAS A STORY WHICH BEGAN
> ONCE UPON A TIME THERE

In *The Floating Opera*, Todd Andrews *had* a story to tell, however
much his philosophical nihilism might have gotten into the way.

For every painful step made in terms of narrative progress,
there was likely to be at least one backward and two to the side.
Like *End Of The Road*, it was a smack at Camus & Co., with comic
twists replacing Existential seriousness. Things turn grimmer, however, when both audiences and the capacity for "story" begin to
run out. Writing blocks—and *talk* about writing blocks—become a
strident concern. As the narrator of "Anonmymiad" puts it:

> By the seventh jug, after effusions of religious narrative, ribald
> tale-cycles, verse-dramas, comedies of manners, and what-all, I had
> begun to run out of world and material—though not of ambition, for
> I could still delight in the thought of my amphorae floating to the

wide world's shores, being discovered by who knew whom, salvaged from the deep, their contents deciphered and broadcast to the ages. Even when, in black humors, I imagined my *opera* sinking, undiscovered (for all I could tell, none might've got past the rocks of my island), or found but untranslated or translated but ignored, I could yet console myself that Zeus at least, or Poseidon, read my heart's record.[5]

Later he imagines his tale afloat, in a passage which sounds like Todd Andrews in Grecian drag:

There, my tale's afloat. I like to imagine it drifting, age after age, while the generations float, sing, love, expire. Now, perhaps, it bumps the very wharfpiles of Mycenae, where my fatal voyage began. Now it passes a hairsbreath from the unknown man or woman whose heart, of all hearts in the world, it could speak fluentest, most balmly-- but they are too preoccupied to hear it. (p. 200)

When a collection of apparently random material finds a home between hard covers, it is hardly surprising that the visions of a unifying principle begin to dance through critical heads. Richard Hauck, for example, sees a title like *Lost In The Funhouse* as "a metaphor for the artist's ambiguous position. . . a 'sequence' of related short stories, some previously published, but the whole arranged loosely as an exercise in the problems the absurd creator as storyteller faces." For all the foot-shuffling self-consciousness, there is a method to Barth's particular madness, a rationale for even the most outrageous puns. "My tale's afloat," the disembodied voice of "Anonymiad" shouts-- in a section of that story called (significantly enough) *Tailpiece*. As I have already suggested, the dovetailing of terms like *opera, floating, craft* (both as "boat" and "narrative skill") point backward-- to Todd Andrews and his unfinished boats.

Moreover, the book has internal unities as well: the first full "story" of the collection is "Night-Sea Journey", a tale of an introspective sperm in existential search of an ovum. The "birth" which presumably creates an Ambrose (the Joycean Artist done here in comic lampoon) ultimately becomes the exhausted voice in "Anonymiad". The " 'Love!' " which provides a climax for "Night-Sea Journey" becomes the thread which ties the multileveled stories in "Menelaiad" together and effectively separates the architect of funhouses [i.e. the author] from the "lovers" who enjoy them. Other unities wander "will-we nill-we" through the text, coming at the central problem of how-to-tell-a-story via tape, print and a variety of combinations. Ambrose may not hold *Lost In The Funhouse* together in quite the ways George Willard or Nick Adams do for *Winesburg, Ohio* and *In Our Time*, but the desperate playfulness of his avatars creates much the same effect.

If one is what Barth calls a "comic nihilist," there is no task more appropriate than that of holding off death with a well-wrought story. More and more, it is Scheherazade who emerges as his Muse. At one point in "Life Story," the narrator (a writer with a characteristically reflexive block) wonders:

> Why is it L wondered with mild disgust that both K and M for example choose to write such stuff when life is so sweet and painful and full of such a variety of people, places, situations, and activities other than self-conscious and after all rather blank introspection? Why is it N wondered et cetera that both M and O et cetera when the world is in such parlous explosive case? Why et cetera et cetera when the word, which was in the beginning, is now evidently nearing the end of its road? [e.g. yet another retrospective pun on an earlier Barth novel, *The End Of The Road*] Am I being strung out in this ad-libitum fashion I wondered merely to keep my author from the pistol? What sort of story is it whose drama lies always in the next frame out? If Sinbad sinks it's Scheherazade who drowns; whose neck one wonders is on the line? (p. 120-121)

"Menlaiad" is Barth's attempt to outdo the stories-within-stories we associate with Scheherazade and *A Thousand And One Nights*. Protean figures (one thinks of Burlingame in *Sot-Weed Factor* or the heroic puzzles of paternity surrounding *Giles Goat-Boy*) provide much of the fluid relativity and con-man humor in Barth's earlier work. What Ralph Ellison feared in *Invisible Man*— that is, the chaos Rhinehartism represents—Barth embraces with comic gusto. The quack doctor in *The End Of The Road* calls the phenomenon "mythotherapy"—an exercise in conscious role-playing—and offers it as a sure-fire antidote to existential ennui. But in "Menelaiad," holding onto Proteus himself is the problem:

> " ' "Hard tale to hold onto this," declared my pooped spouse,' Odysseus'—or Nestor's—son agreed." But what out-wandering hero ever journeyed a short straight line, arrived at his beginning till the end?" ' " Harder yet to hold onto Proteus, I must have dozed, as I mused and fretted, thought myself yet again enhorsed or bridal-chambered, same old dream, woke up clutching nothing. It was late. I was

rooted with fatigue. I held on." (' ') "To?" (' ') "Nothing. You were back on deck, the afternoon sank, I heard sailors suffawing, shore-birds cackled, the sun set grinning in the winish sea, still I held on, saying of and to me: 'Menelaus is a fool, mortal hugging immortality. Men laugh, the gods mock, he's chimaera, a horned full. What is it he clutches? Why can't he let go? What trick have you played him, Eidothea, a stranger in your country?' I might've quit, but my cursed fancy whispered: 'Proteus has turned into the air. Or else. . .' " ' "

Hold onto yourself, Menelaus. (p. 143)

"Menelaiad" must be *heard* to be believed. Several years ago Barth "performed" the story—with audio-visual aids and first-rate the-atrics—at a number of academic watering holes along the lecture circuit. The stories-within-stories, speakers-within-speakers contin-ued to interlock like an elaborate Chinese puzzle, but the central theme—that love *received* (rather than "given") is a mystery which introspection can destroy—comes through all the comedy with great force.

At this point an intrusion on my part may help to clarify Barth's penchant to do the same thing. Our most interesting literary criticism often comes at us from oblique angles, especially where Post-Modernist writers are concerned. In his recent novel, *Scoring*, Dan Greenburg makes a very pertinent aside:

> I think the way to really get to know any character in a book is to peek into his life when he thinks there is no one looking. Let us accept for a moment the notion that I am willing to let you peek into my life in such a manner. I'm not, of course, but what I *am* willing to let you see would satisfy your most voyeuristic appetites, if not downright turn your stomach. Six and a half years of intensive psycho-analysis have made me a master of the seemingly-painful-but-ulti-mately-calculating confession, Such tricky candor, as Messrs. Mailer, Roth and Podhoretz well know, is not only therapeutic but self serving: if I tell you an anecdote that makes me seem an insensitive boor, and if I then call your attention to how insensitive and how boorish I am, you may be so disarmed by my frankness and by my self-awareness that you forget for a moment that the admission makes me no less an insensitive boor.[7]

"Confessional" writing and the ultra-reflexive mode share much, not the least of which is that dead-end known as self-parody. What Greenburg calls "tricky candor" may be highly selective (in fact, the things Messrs. Mailer, Roth and Podhoretz leave *out* are often more revealing than the things they include), but that is how built-in victories are made. And, too, normal expectations play a part; after all, if a "dirty little secret" is about to be unwrapped, it is hardly good form to quibble at either the carpet or the figure which emerges. Of course, competition has a way of raising the stakes in such ventures. Novelists are not the only ones to trade on bruised childhoods and battered marriages. Poets and playwrights want their share of that gooey pie called success. That escalation will set in is as inevitable as those portraits in the grotesque which have become standard operating procedure for writers in the 1960's.

Barth has been particularly effective is exploiting one corollary of this proposition. While he steadfastly shuns the directly autobiographical, there is confessional movement on other fronts. He is a writer who compulsively calls our attention to the fact that he is a writer, albeit one laboring under a severe "block." In this way not only does the writing (or, to be more correct, the *non*-writing) of fiction becomes its own subject—and the occasion for endlessly comic shop talk. Old-fashioned ground rules like "plot" or even narrative forward motion fly out the window. Even the best of this reflexive bunch—Borges, Barthelme, Beckett—sometimes strain to make all the lexical dazzle fit onto such a flimsy canvas. Like confectioner's sugar, a little goes a long way.

Since *Lost In The Funhouse* Barth has been a tireless laborer in this particular vineyard. Consider, for example, the following bit of reflexive footwork from the title story:

> The action of conventional dramatic narrative may represented by a diagram called Freitag's Triangle:

> Or more accurately by a variant of that diagram:

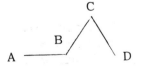

in which AB represents the exposition, B the introduction of conflict, BC the "rising action," complication, or development of the conflict, CD the denouement, or resolution of the conflict. While there is no reason to regard this pattern as an absolute necessity, like many other conventions it became conventional because great numbers of people over many years learned by trial and error that it was effective; one ought not to forsake it, therefore, unless one wishes to forsake as well the effect of drama or has clear cause to feel that deliberate violation of the "normal" pattern can better can better (sic) effect that effect. This can't go on much longer; it can go on forever. He [i.e. Ambrose?; Barth?] died telling stories to himself in the dark. . . (p. 95)

Much of this sounds like the sort of advice Barth might give to a fiction-writers' workshop. On the other hand, it, too, might be a parody—of somebody else's well-meaning pronouncements to somebody else's class. No matter. The paralysing effect is the same. Without a real *story* to tell, one is reduced to a blow-by-blow description of the process.

In *Chimera*, Barth breaks into the "Bellerophoniad" to bring us the "good news" he has discovered:

'Since myths themselves are among other things poetic distillations of our ordinary psychic experience and therefore point always to daily reality, to write realistic fictions which point always to mythic archetypes is in my opinion to take the wrong end of the mythopoeic stick, however meritorious such fictions may be in other respects. . .'[8]

Barth probably has a contemporary novel like John Updike's *Centaur* in mind here, although such Modernist classics as *Ulysses* and *The Waste Land* also share honored places at the wrong end of this mythic *shtick*. But we need no English professor from Johns Hopkins to tell us that mythic figures like Chimera or Bellerophon retain a potent power. Barth's former colleague at Buffalo—Leslie Fiedler—had already made the point in spades.

What Barth adds to the ongoing discussion about myth and modern literature (one thinks, inevitably, of Eliot's seminal essay "*Ulysses*, Order and Myth" which may have said all that was *really* necessary) is a gamsy contempt for print, for readers and, possibly, for himself. As his persona puts it in *Lost In The Funhouse*'s "Like Story":

The reader! You dogged, uninsultable, print-oriented bastard, it's

you I'm addressing, who else, from inside this monstrous fiction.
You've read me this far, then? Even this far? For what discreditable
motive? How is it you don't go to a movie, watch TV, stare at a wall,
play tennis with a friend, make amorous advance to the person who
comes to your mind when I speak of amorous advances? Can nothing
surfiet, saturate you, turn you off? What's your shame? (p. 127)

Which brings me to my own title "The Teller Who Swallowed
His Tale". The image I have in mind, of course, is that of a snake
eating its own tail. Leslie Fiedler likes to talk about *Giles Goat--
Boy* as a novel out to blow up Modernist assumptions about Art
from the inside. "Implosions" (to use a phrase made popular
by the popularizing Marshall McLuhan) comes to mind immediately, but an editorially wielded blue pencil might have been
more to the artistic point. In short, Barth is not so much the
great destroyer of Modernism— exaggerating its faults through
comic excess and parody— than he is the devourer of his own
talents. The principle that "fiction must acknowledge its ficti-
ousness and metaphoric invalidity" might be an interesting thesis,
even the subject for an academic symposium, but, baldly stated,
it is a poor narrative line on which to hang a story. Besides, Modernism had pushed the self-destruct button long before the days
of John Barth. It had *always* been there, just on the other side
of literary coins like *The Waste Land* or *Ulysses*.

Notes

1   Barth himself admits the phrase is self-consciously chic and certainly overused. Nonetheless, since its first appearance in *Atlantic* (August 1967) a great many other writers have rushed in to tell us that *they* are pooped-out too.

2   John Barth, "The Literature of Exhaustion" included in Marcus Klein, ed., *The American Novel Since World War II* (New York: Fawcett, 1969), p. 275.

3   Like Todd Andrews, John Dowell suffers from an ill-defined "heart" condition and he too is more trickster than reliable narrator.

4   John Barth, The Floating Opera (New York: Avon, 1956), p. 9. Subsequent references to *The Floating Opera* are to this edition and pagination is given parenthetically.

5   John Barth, *Lost In The Funhouse* (New York: Doubleday & Co., 1968), p. 194.

6   Richard Hauck, *A Cheerful Nihilism* (Bloomington: Indiana University Press, 1971). p. 203.

7   Dan Greenburg, *Scoring* (New York: Doubleday & Co., 1972), pp. 19-20.

8   John Barth, *Chimera* (New York: Random House, 1972), p. 199.

VI

Fire And Ice: The Radical Cuteness Of Kurt Vonnegut, Jr.

> *Some say the world will end*
> *in fire;*
> *Some say in ice.   .   .*

—Robert Frost

For a Modernist like James Joyce, the figure of Prometheus dovetailed defiance, creativity and victimhood into a highly attractive metaphor. The forces of family, church and state urge the young Stephen to "apologize" and then threaten him with dreadful punishment if he does not: "the eagles will come and pull out his eyes." Literary martyrdom is all.

The Post-Modernist, on the other hand, fashions his manifesto from slimmer goods. Unlike those thick books - *Ulysses, The Magic Mountain, Remembrance Of Things Past* - which "prove" the inner life is all, he prefers that blank space which Marshall McLuhan assures us is both the medium and the "massage". And the Post-Modernist's emblem swings in an arc from Pluto (God of the Underworld) to Persephone (the captive allowed occasional visits to the earth above). No writer in the sixties epitomizes this tendency toward boom-and-bust more than Kurt Vonnegut, Jr. He is the boozy and mustachioed, Pall Mall puffing hero of the young and the center of an underground cult that has lived very much *above* the surface for the last few years. Of course, America makes life tough for its underground heroes and Vonnegut has had to contend with all the trappings: a teaching position at Harvard, a cover photo on *Life* and a film version of *Slaughterhouse-Five.* No doubt commercials - in the style of Stan Freberg - will be next, trumpeting the virtues of Levi slacks from Tralfamadore.

His first novel, *Player Piano* (1952), was quickly lumped

into that pulp-ridden category known as science fiction. It was a fairly predictable slice of futuristic life, complete with a shifty protagonist named Paul Proteus. Had it all happened in a Barth novel (where Protean characters are always at stagecenter) the effect might have stirred more critical waves. Instead Vonnegut—like Kilgore Trout, the unheralded sci-fi writer who serves as his alter ego—enjoyed a share in the cult worship which had surrounded books like Robert Heinlan's *Stranger in a Strange Land.*

In *The Sirens Of Titan* (1959) Vonnegut introduced Winston Niles Rumfoord and the comic nihilism we associate with the planet Tralfamadore. For the purist, here is Vonnegut at his unself-conscious best, plying his wares as a writer of sub-genre. Rather than, say, the solipsistic worlds-within-worlds one expects in Modernist fiction, Vonnegut inverts the process, projecting endless planets-within-planets and neatly reducing all human history (Stonehenge, the Great Wall, the League of Nations palace) to a sci-fi footnote. For Stephen Dedalus, history was a deterministic nightmare from which he tried to awake, one which grew more terrifying with each scholastic allusion. But while the baggage that is history may have been a heavy burden for Joyce or Eliot, it is a lightweight affair for Vonnegut. And all too often *The Sirens Of Titan* smacks of a wildly comic "Ozymandias" on one hand and a cheap shot on the other.

With *Mother Night* (1961), however, Vonnegut begins to inch toward more congenial, more *literary* material. There is a cunning in history, particularly where the fiction writer is concerned. The dividing line between that consensus about history known as Modernism and the affair we call Post-Modernism is World War II. By now the aftermath of World War I is a matter of record and one need not rehearse the energies which toppled governments and traditional modes of fiction alike. It is sufficient to say that not *all* the explosions occurred along the Maginot line; as Yeats and other Modernists understood, the center had been falling apart for some time. But the "new fiction" felt itself equal to the task of seeing modern life steadily and whole. The air was thick with competing manifestoes—and even a few giants with the talent required to make good on heady promises.

World War II and its aftermath was another matter. Certain initiations—that modern warfare is technological and anti-heroic or

or that despair and disillusionment are fairly predictable by-products—were precluded in advance. Pound and Hemingway (to say
nothing of Remarque) had proved already that the language of a
recruitment poster lies. In short, at least *some* of the objections to
war could have been eloquently voiced when draftees received their
notices. Of course, World War II had some moral wrinkles that the
First War lacked. One shorthand way of putting it might be this:
the decade after 1917 loosed hedonism onto an already weakening
Victorian stage, while the world after Auschwitz cried out for moral
reappraisal and a crash course in situation ethics. Perhaps that is
why significant fiction about World War II has been a continuing
problem for the contemporary novelist, rather than a subject to be
exhausted within that ten year statute of limitations usually applied
to "war" novels.

   Mother Night is filled with those dazzling reversals and artful
dodges that make for what I call radical cuteness. In the fifties
Salinger & Co. were the major stockholders and sensitive children
seemed to be their stock in trade. But in the national smugness
which permeated that decade, what better time to wonder about
the inherent phoniness of prep school life or the dangers of competing for a part in the college play? It all looked innocent enough
and, after all, innocence is the name of the game for American
writers. Vonnegut brings something of that spirit to the troubled
sixties, although, this time, the subject strikes one as demanding
more than even a radical cuteness can supply. In his "Introduction"
Vonnegut suggests that

> This is the only story of mine whose moral I know. I don't think it's
> a marvelous moral: I simply happen to know what it is: We are what
> we pretend to be, so we must be careful about what we pretend to
> be.[1]

Art and pretense are inextricably bound; indeed, Harry Campbell
is emblematic of those who "served evil too openly and good too
secretly, the crime of his times". He is, in short, the much beleaguered Formalist, a man of Art rather than social conscience.
Vonnegut tests out the limitations of such aesthetic theories by
casting Campbell as a

> .   .   . fairly successful playwright, writing in the language in which
> I write best, German. I had one play, "The Goblet," running in both
> Dresden and Berlin. Another play of mine, "The Snow Rose" was

then in production in Berlin. I had just finished a third one, "Seventy Times Seven." All three plays were medieval romances, about as political as chocolate *eclairs*. (p. 37)

But while *Das Reich der Zwei* (that "Nation of Two" which Campbell plans to celebrate in his next play by showing "how a pair of lovers in a world gone mad could survive by being loyal only to a nation composed of themselves"), the *Third* Reich replaces such gentle dreams with nightmares that are all too real.

To be sure, Campbell is the con-man conned, the victimizer who is also the victim. No matter how grotesque or patently absurd his Nazi propaganda becomes, it never tumbles into parody; the ironies always manage to escape his audience. Even Harry Campbell, Jr. is no match for the insanity of the world. He is fated to be forever misunderstood, the hate artist/allied spy who finds life on the edges intolerable. As one German puts it:

".   . . you could never have served the enemy as well as you served us," he said. "I realized that almost all the ideas that I hold now, that make me unashamed of anything I may have felt or done as a Nazi, came not from Hitler, not from Goebbels, not from Himmler—but from you." He took my hand. "You alone kept me from concluding that Germany had gone insane." (pp. 80-81)

Thus, Vonnegut gives that turn of the screw called Illusion/Reality yet another twist, albeit one which stacks Art against Life and gives the moral questions in between short shrift. In such a moral vacuum the leather straps of suitcases or an execution tend to look alike:

"When Hoess was hanged," he [i.e. his guard, Bernard Mengel] told me, "the strap around his ankles—I put that on and made it tight."

"Did that give you a lot of satisfaction?" I said.

"No," he said, "I was like almost everybody who came through that war."

"What do you mean?" I said.

"I got so I couldn't feel anything," said Mengel. "Every job was a job to do, and no job was any better or any worse than any other."

"After we finished hanging Hoess," Mengel said to me, "I packed up my clothes to go home. The catch on my suitcase was broken, so I buckled it shut with a big leather strap. Twice within an hour I did the very same job—once to Hoess and once to my suitcase. Both jobs felt about the same." (pp. 24-25)

Vonnegut paces *Mother Night* with short, punchy "chapters" of this sort, usually under four pages in length and geared to some darkly comic punch line. But the combined weight—there are no less than forty five chapters—breeds its own brand of repetitive boredom. Unlike the alternating vignettes and full-blown stories of, say, Ernest Hemingway's *In Our Time* (where the blank space pays its aesthetic way), writers like Vonnegut or Brautigan merely grow insistent about the cutely thin.

If Mengel's leather straps have a way of cancelling each other out, so do the sharply divided political teams which surround Harry Campbell. But it hardly matters. Minor characters, both Right and Left, wear the same face. And in the escalating grotesquery that pits a super-communist like George Kraft against a super-fascist like J. D. Jones, blurring replaces moral consequence. Such is the peril of disguise in a world where action speaks louder than intention and each man wears the uniform of an ideology.

Moreover, Vonnegut's point about the Nazi doppelgänger within each of us, his insistence that each apparent Self has a concealed counterpart just underneath the skin, makes good—all *too* good—on a notion contemporary fiction inherits from earlier works like "Heart of Darkness" or *Women In Love*. According to Tony Tanner, this uncertain relationship between surface and hidden content is directly related to a comparable uncertainty about the various relationships in *Mother Night*. The intimation is that "we may become our own cover-stories" and, furthermore, that "there may be a more authentic self in the invented ones."[2]

Campbell's suicide suggests that this is certainly true in *his* case. The propaganda he broadcasts is more effective than the "secret codes" he secretly transmits. But Vonnegut forecloses the tragic possibilities of "secret sharing" in advance. Campbell is denied a context which might make the moment of his insight meaningful. In a scenario without consensus villians and authentic evil, the Harry Campbell, Jrs., can only look pathetic.

Vonnegut's next novel—*Cat's Cradle* (1963)—tests out the dark connections between scientific research and unbridled play. For Dr. Felix Hoeniker, inventor of the atom bomb and ice-nine, there is a gamsy quality about both. The scientific apocalypse moves on one level; the mythic religion of Bokonism moves on another. But as Newt Hoeniker (who was introduced to cat's cradles on the day the first atomic bomb exploded) puts it:

> "For maybe a hundred thousand years or more, grownups have been waving tangles of string in their children's faces. . . . No wonder kids grow up crazy. A cat's cradle is nothing but a bunch of X's between somebody's hands, and the little kids look and look at all those X's. . ."
>
> "And?"
>
> "No damn cat, and no damn cradle."[3]

In *Mother Night* Vonnegut warns against pretenses which have a way of becoming existential realities. *Cat's Cradle* looks at life from the other side of the coin. "Call me Jonah"—unlucky scapegoat rather than outlawed wanderer—provides the opening note. However, this time the quest is not for a symbolically charged Moby Dick, but that ultimate "whiteness of whiteness" called *ice-nine*. Campbell dreams of a traumatically interrupted play called "A Nation of Two"; the narrator of *Cat's Cradle* projects a very different sort of book, one entitled *The Day The World Ended*. The Nazi Holocaust, the nuclear apocalypse—strange subjects even for the blackest humorist. Nonetheless, Vonnegut's work manages to transpose high seriousness into a new and wildly comic key. Moral questions exhaust themselves quickly, with radical cuteness providing a new alternative for what "was to be a Christian book." (p. 11) As the first sentence in the mythical *Books Of Bokonon* puts it: "All of the true things I am about to tell you are shameless lies." (p. 14) The moral lesson of *Mother Night* is replaced by a narrator who warns:

> Anyone unable to understand how a useful religion can be founded on lies will not understand this book either. (p. 14)

Both Felix Hoeniker and the founder of Bokonism share a child-like fascination with the possibilities of play. The Research Laboratory of the General Forge and Foundry Company is devoted to pure "thinking" and purified research. In such a world men do not concern themselves with

> . . . looking for a better cigarette filter or a softer face tissue or a longer-lasting house paint, God help us. Everybody talks about research and practically nobody in this country's doing it. We're one of the few companies that actually hires men to do pure research. When most other companies brag about their research, they're talking about industrial hack technicians who wear white coats, work out of cookbooks, and dream up an improved windshield wiper for next year's automobile." (p. 35)

The moral implications which had been suspended in Campbell's aesthetic of pure Art are reconstituted in Felix Hoeniker's credo of "pure science." When a Marine general (tired of wallowing in the mud) brings his "problem" to their Research Laboratory, Hoeniker plays Faust with vengeance. As Dr. Breed puts it:

> "In his playful way, and *all* his ways were playful, Felix suggested that there might be a single grain of something—even a microscopic grain—that could make infinite expanses of muck, marsh, creeks, pools, quicksand, and mire as solid as this desk. . . . One Marine could carry more than enough of the stuff to free an armored division bogged down in the everglades. According to Felix, one Marine could carry enough of the stuff to do that under the nail of his little finger."

> "That's impossible."

> "You would say so, I would say so—practically everybody would say so. To Felix, in his playful way, it was entirely possible. The miracle of Felix—and I sincerely hope you'll put this in your book somewhere— was that he always approached old puzzles as though they were brand new." (p. 37)

Ice-nine develops from a similar cast of mind.[4] For Vonnegut, scientists like Felix Hoeniker, makers of new religions and writers of science fiction (Kilgore Trout) have the child-like sensibility necessary to "murder and create" in the Post-Modern world. *Cat's Cradle* pitches the battle between the all too real effects of *ice-nine* and illusionary power of Bokonism.

The respective teams are etched with broad-ax strokes: "*busy, busy, busy,* is what we Bokonists whisper whenever we think of how complicated and unpredictable the machinery of life really is." vs. the world around them which ends in *ice-nine. Cat's Cradle* is "cold pastoral" at its ultimate. The "soft pipes" of Angela's frozen clarinet "play on," but only to that inner ear Bokonists apparently have. Thumbing one's nose at "You know Who" is, therefore, an appropriate gesture, the final sentence of Bokonon's calypso epic.

With *God Bless You, Mr. Rosewater* (1965) Vonnegut tests out the limitations of sanity via the zany ways in which Rosewater's guilt (he had killed three unarmed firemen during the War) are sublimated into escalating drunkenness, charitable foundations, science fiction and a simplified ethic of universal kindness. Terry Southern's *The Magic Christian* (1960) had covered much of the same ground earlier, but Vonnegut adds some predictable wrinkles of his own. For example, Rosewater once addressed a convention of science fiction writers (who meet, by the way, in a motel in Milford, Pa.) with the following bit of good cheer:

> "I love you sons of bitches. . . . You're all I read any more. You're the only ones who'll talk about the *really* terrific changes going on, the only ones crazy enough to know that life is a space voyage, and not a short one either, but one that'll last for billions of years. You're the only ones with guts enough to *really* care about the future, who *really* notice what machines do to us, what wars do to us, what cities do to us, what big, simple ideas do to us, what tremendous misunderstandings, mistakes, accidents and catastrophes do to us. You're the only ones zany enough to agonize over time and distances without limit, over mysteries that will never die, over the fact that we are right now determining whether the space voyage for the next billion years or so is going to be Heaven or Hell!"[6]

Of course, even Rosewater admits that "science-fiction writers couldn't write for sour apples," but at least they grappled with the important questions. Kilgore Trout's numerical equivalent of Hamlet's problem—a book called 2BRO2B—merges with the novel's overriding question.

ROSEWATER FOUNDATION

HOW CAN WE HELP

YOU?

The result is a million dollar version of Nathanael West's *Miss*

Lonelyhearts, although, this time, the suffering is sent in by phone:

> "My kidneys hurt me all day, Mr. Rosewater. They feel like a red-hot cannonball of electricity was going through them real slow, and just turning round and round, with poisoned razorblades sticking out it." (p. 59)

And like West's doomed protagonist, Rosewater takes on their trouble. His track record (significantly called the *Domesday Book*) is filled with cryptic notations which combine efficiency with the playfulness of a Kilgore Trout:

> "Sherman Wesley Little," wrote Eliot. "*Indy*, Su-TDM-LO-V2-W3k3-K2CP-RF $300." Decoded, this meant that Little was from Indianapolis, was a suicidal tool-and-die maker who had been laid off, veteran of the Second World War with a wife and three children, the second child suffering from cerebral palsy. Eliot awarded him a Rosewater Fellowship of $300. (pp. 77-78)

In short, Eliot becomes an artist, one devoted to the possibilities of unbridled charity and unbounded love. If Vonnegut's novels each contain some splash of moral tonic, *God Bless You, Mr. Rosewater*'s may be the simplest of all: "God damn it, you've got to be kind." (p. 93) Eliot Rosewater devotes himself to those who

> ". . . can't even care about themselves any more—because they have no *use*. The factory, the farms, the mines across the river—they're almost completely automatic now. And America doesn't even need these people for war—not any more. Sylvia—I'm going to be an artist."
>
> "An artist?"
>
> "I'm going to love these discarded Americans, even though they're useless and unattractive. *That* is going to be my work of art." (p. 36)

And his final gesture—acknowledging "that every child in Rosewater County said to be mine *is* mine, regardless of blood type" (p. 190)—completes the novel's mythic structure of comic wastelands and comic redeemers. Eliot Rosewater raises "his tennis racket as though it were a magic wand," and all of us—however desperate—are told to "be fruitful and multiply."

Slaughterhouse-Five (1969) is largely an attempt at synthesis.

In a sense, the thematic strands and zany characters of earlier novels constitute a warm-up for the *real* stuff Vonnegut wants to get off his chest. Like Eliot Rosewater, Billy Pilgrim is a victim of World War II. But while Rosewater's comic obsession with fire departments is a response to his inadvertent murder of three people, Billy Pilgrim is a survivor of the Dresden fire-bombing which killed 135,000 innocent civilians. In coming to terms with his own memories of that event, Vonnegut explores the assets and liabilities of madness itself. Not merely as a Black Humorist out to outdo the headlines of a world gone absurd, but, rather, as a man driven to the very borders of insanity and beyond in a search for health. *Cat's Cradle* ended in apocalyptic death; *Slaughterhouse-Five* begins there. However, even thumbing one's nose—confident that Bokonon would approve—is no longer quite enough. According to Auden, "mad Ireland" hurt a Modernist like Yeats into poetry. The Post-Modern world drives Vonnegut to Tralfamadore. There Billy Pilgrim learns to accept death as an event without genuine import:

> . . . I learned on Tralfamadore that when a person dies he only *appears* to die. He is still very much alive in the past, so it is very silly for people to cry at his funeral. All moments, past, present, and future, always have existed, always will exist. The Tralfamadorians can look at all the different mountains just the way we can look at a stretch of the Rocky Mountains, for instance. They can see how permanent all the moments are, and they can look at any moment that interests them. It is just an illusion we have here on earth that one moment follows another one, like beads of a string, and that once a moment is gone it is gone forever.

> "When a Tralfamadorian sees a corpse, all he thinks is that the dead person is in bad condition at that particular moment, but that the same person is just fine in plenty of other moments. Now, when I myself hear that somebody is dead, I simply shrug and say what the Tralfamadorians say about dead people, which is 'So it goes.' "[7](p. 23)

Once again, Vonnegut's narrator is out to write a book, one which actually "happened, more or less." (p. 1) But, this time, there are promises given in advance and the most perplexing "moral" of all:

> . . . "Mary," I said, "I don't think this book of mine is ever going to be finished. I must have written five thousand pages by now, and thrown them all away. If I ever do finish it, though, I give you my word of honor: there won't be a part for Frank Sinatra or John Wayne."[8]

'I tell you what," I said. "I'll call it 'The Children's Crusade.' "

She was my friend after that. (p. 13)

The moral, of course, is "So it goes," a phrase ritually chanted after anything dies. The death of a fictional character, champagne bubbles or six million Jews generates an identical response on Tralfamadore. So it goes. *All* deaths are equally absurd, equally meaningless. Billy Pilgrim—Bunyanesque and "unstuck in time"— has been privy to the only truth which can deal with an apocalyptic event like the Dresden fire-storm. And, too, Billy's radical sense of time gives the prayer of St. Francis ("God grant me the serenity to accept the things I cannot change, courage to change the things I can, and the wisdom to tell the difference.") a new twist:

Among the things Billy Pilgrim could not change were the past, the present and the future. (p. 52)

In the early 1960's Joseph Heller's *Catch-22* (1961) championed the cause of raw survival against those bureaucratic forces which kill people in the name of "catch-22." Gone were the notions that war is a gloryless Hell (Remarque's *All Quiet On The Western Front*) or that philosophical/moral issues are involved (Mailer's *The Naked And The Dead*). Heller pitches life on Pianosa at a time when the war, for all practical purposes, is over. The moral issues of democracy vs. fascism are suspended and men like Yossarian simply want to get out alive. Vonnegut's novel may cast a backward glance at Dresden, but, like Heller, he writes both *for* and *to* a sensibility of the sixties. Interestingly enough, *Catch-22* and *Slaughterhouse-Five*—which strike me as having polar visions—receive equal praise from that highly vocal lobby called the young. If nothing else, the agonizing spectre of Snowden's death suggests that war is a grisly business and "catch-22" a highly efficient, albeit comic, way of greasing the gallows. Protest, rather than cosmic acceptance, is its keystone. That a Yossarian (or perhaps more to the point, an Orr) should shrug his shoulders and say "So it goes" is unthinkable.

In the world of *Catch-22*, paranoia and a heightened sense of reality are indistinguishable. As the old canard would have it: "If you can keep your head when all about you are losing theirs—then obviously you have not grasped the true seriousness of the situation." On the other hand, *Slaughterhouse-Five* takes a very different tack:

> "So—" said Billy gropingly, "I suppose that the idea of preventing war on Earth is stupid, too."
>
> "Of course."
>
> "But you *do* have a peaceful planet here."
>
> "Today we do. On others days we have wars as horrible as any you've ever seen or read about. There isn't anything we can do about them, so we simply don't look at them. We ignore them. We spend eternity looking at pleasant moments—like today at the zoo. Isn't this a nice moment."
>
> "Yes."
>
> "That's one thing Earthlings might learn to do, if they tried hard enough; ignore the awful times, and concentrate on the good ones."
>
> "Um," said Billy Pilgrim. (pp. 101-102)

As Eliot Rosewater (who reappears in *Slaughterhouse-Five* along with other characters from the Vonnegut stable like Bernard O'Hare, Harry Campbell, Jr. and Kilgore Trout) tells his psychiatrist: "I think you guys are going to have to come up with a lot of wonderful *new* lies, or people just aren't going to want to go on living." (pp. 87-88) The remark could stand as a convenient epigraph for Vonnegut's canon. According to Rosewater, *The Brothers Karamazov* "isn't *enough* any more; for people trying to re-invent themselves and their universe (i.e. Eliot Rosewater, Billy Pilgrim and, presumably, Vonnegut's readers) "science fiction was a big help." (p. 87)

All this is not to suggest, however, that Vonnegut skirts horror entirely. The same radical cuteness which de-fused the seriousness of death on Tralfamadore also inverts war movies with chilling effect:

> He [i.e. Billy] came slightly unstuck in time, saw the late movie backwards, then forwards again. It was a movie about American bombers in the Second World War and the gallant men who flew them. Seen backwards by Billy, the story went like this:

American planes, full of holes and wounded men and corpses took off backwards from a airfield in England. Over France, a few German fighter planes flew at them backwards, sucked bullets and shell fragments from some of the planes and crewmen. They did the same for wrecked American bombers on the ground, and those planes flew up backwards to join the formation.

The formation flew backwards over a German city that was in flames. The bombers opened their bomb bay doors, exerted a miraculous magnetism which shrunk the fires, gathered them into cylindrical steel containers, and lifted the containers into the bellies of the planes. The containers were stored neatly in racks. The Germans below had miraculous devices of their own, which were long steel tubes. They used them to suck more fragments from the crewmen and planes. But there were still a few wounded Americans, though, and some of the bombers were in bad repair. Over France, though, German fighters came up again, made everything and everybody as good as new. (pp. 63-64)

And, too, there are scattered vignettes in *Slaughterhouse-Five* which rival Nathanael West at his most grotesque:

". . . You should have seen what I [i.e. Paul Lazzaro] did to a dog one time.   . . Son of a bitch bit me. So I got me some steak, and I got me the spring out of a clock. I cut that spring up in little pieces. I put points on the ends of the pieces. They were sharp as razor blades. I stuck 'em into the steak—way inside. And I went past where they had the dog tied up. He wanted to bit me again. I said to him, 'Come on doggie—let's be friends. Let's not be enemies any more. I'm not mad.' He believed me."

        "He *did*?"

"I threw him the steak. He swallowed it down in one big gulp. I waited around for ten minutes." Now Lazzaro's eyes twinkled. "Blood started coming out of his mouth. He started crying, and he rolled on the ground, as though the knives were on the outside of him instead of on the inside of him. Then he tried to bite out his own insides. I laughed, and I said to him, 'You got the right idea now. Tear your own guts out, boy. That's *me* in there with all those knives.' " So it goes. (pp. 120-121)

But the novel ends in springtime all the same: the wagon outside the slaughterhouse may be "coffin-shaped," but it is also "green." And the birds sing *"Poo-tee-weet?"* to a Billy Pilgrim who has learned that mulling over the pleasant moments is better than brooding about death.

Vonnegut's critics prefer to think of his fables as "deceptively simple," rather than simple-minded. Like Kilgore Trout, Vonnegut spends his artistic time "opening the window and making love to the world." (*Slaughterhouse-Five*, p. 145) And to a generation of the young and would-be young, the message seems to have gotten through. As one recent study of the contemporary novel puts it:

> No novelist in the sixties is more aware of the necessity of exorcising our dreams of death than Kurt Vonnegut, Jr., and no novelist is more avid in his use of the fable form as an exorcising comfort and a loving prod. The dark, tough, apocalyptic quality of Vonnegut's vision results from his hard-minded recognition that we do commit sins against ourselves which need to be exorcized. But he dresses that perception in the fable's soft fabric, moral fibers and all, because he sees love as the proper instrument of exorcism, and the fable as the proper form for the expression of the artist's love.[9]

But the radically cute has a nasty habit of turning into the radically thin. In a world where death cannot be taken seriously, tragic art (like everything else) becomes a cat's cradle. Vonnegut may *console*, but genuine exorcism must be made of sterner stuff. Tralfamadore, pleasant moments and all, hardly constitutes the right turf. Which is to say, critical love letters should be sent by airmail. So it goes.

Notes

1   Kurt Vonnegut, Jr., *Mother Night* (New York: Avon, 1961), v. Subsequent references to *Mother Night* are to this edition and pagination is given parenthetically.

2   Tony Tanner, *City of Words* (New York: Harper & Row, 1971), p. 187. Professor Tanner's chapter entitled "The Uncertain Messenger" remains the best study of Vonnegut's canon to date.

3   Kurt Vonnegut, Jr., *Cat's Cradle* (New York: Dell, 1963), p. 114. Subsequent references to *Cat's Cradle* are to this edition and pagination is given parenthetically.

4   Vonnegut discusses the origins of *ice-nine* in an interview with C. D. B. Bryan entitled "Kurt Vonnegut, Head Bokonist," in the *New York Times Book Review* (6 April 1969), pp. 2, 25.

5   Interestingly enough, Leslie Fiedler, an early and enthusiastic admirer of Vonnegut's work, once addressed a convention of science-fiction writers and judged a competition of their work—although *not* in Milford, Pa.

6   Kurt Vonnegut, Jr., *God Bless You, Mr. Rosewater* (New York: Dell, 1965), p. 18. Subsequent references to *God Bless You, Mr. Rosewater* are to this edition and pagination is given parenthetically.

7   Kurt Vonnegut, Jr., *Slaughterhouse-Five* (New York: Dell, 1969), p. 23. Subsequent references to *Slaughterhouse-Five* are to this edition and pagination is given parenthetically.

8   In one of those curious moments where Life imitates Art, the film version of *Slaughterhouse-Five* made good on Vonnegut's promise. There is no part for either Frank Sinatra or John Wayne. On the other hand, when they filmed *Catch-22* Henry Fonda refused an offer to play the role of Major Major, a man burdened by his uncanny resemblance to Henry Fonda.

9   Raymond Olderman, *Beyond the Waste Land* (New Haven: Yale University Press, 1972), p. 189.

VII

The Mixed Chords of David Madden's CASSANDRA SINGING

The annual gathering of the Modern Language Association is an unlikely place to meet a novelist, especially if he is not scheduled to give one of those inspirational talks which sometimes dot the scholarly program. Yet there he was—at a session sponsored by the New University Conference; the exact topic escapes me, but David Madden was unforgettable. Perhaps the wholesale assault on literature had conjured up Formalist memories from the days when he was the *Kenyon Review*'s Assistant Editor. Perhaps the critic in him (books on Wright Morris and James Cain) spoke to scholarly conferences gone haywire. In any event, he began to talk about Eastern Kentucky and the folk who provided the raw material for his latest novel, *Cassandra Singing* (1969). The lack of communication that resulted might have been the envy of a Samuel Beckett. Madden found himself shouted down, berated for writing fiction while the slag heaps and mine owners continued to exploit real (as opposed to effetely "fictional") people. No matter that most of the audience had never *seen* a coal mine (much less worked in one) or had ever talked to a *living* coal miner. Questions about literature rapidly boiled down to: "whose class interests does it serve?" And Madden—slightly balding and too short for proletarian stock—was on the wrong side. His accent may have had the hint of a hillbilly twang, but the echoes of Brooks and Warren came through much stronger.

I mentioned this not so much for its biographical value (Madden's difficulties, after all, were hardly an isolated case in 1971) but because *Cassandra Singing* shares all the assets and liabilities that accrue when an author is that much maligned thing we call a "man of letters." As Madden himself proudly catalogs:

> During the prolonged struggle with its massive raw material [*Cassandra Singing*], I was able, fortunately, to write and publish many other

things. I wrote six one-act and three long plays which have won prizes, production and publication; I wrote three novels, two of which were published; fifteen poems—ten published; twenty short stories—thirteen published; a book-length critical study of the novelist Wright Morris—also published; and fifty long book reviews.[1]

But *Cassandra Singing* was never far away. From one compulsive draft to the next, Madden refined and redrew his characters in an attempt to get some very native things off his chest. The result has all the energy and excess we associate with second-rate theater— that is, the cords do not quite tie, the themes do not quite gell, but the "failure" is more interesting than many a "success."

The novel announces one of its central concerns in the opening sentence: "The backfiring of a motorcycle as it roared over the loose planks of the swinging bridge opened Lone's eyes."[2] Lone has had his eyes opened—both literally and figuratively—by Boyd Weaver and the free-wheeling motorcycle life he represents. As Cassie puts it, when Lone rolls a cigarette in imitation of Boyd: "Smokin' ain't all. Taught you how to ride a 'sickle, how to stay out late, how to drink Falstaff" (p. 13). The brand name is a legitimate bit of local color, but much in the Boyd/Lone relationship suggests parallels to Falstaff and Prince Hal. The Lone of nickname—rather than the Wayne of birth—is the alienated protagonist of Madden's novel. The McDaniel family has pinned its hopes on him, and the responsibility becomes a heavy weight. Boyd Weaver, a motorcycle, and the open road make for attractive alternatives. However, just as the motorcycle backfires in ominous foreshadowing, so, too, do Lone's hopes for an uncluttered and independent life. Boyd is an interlude for Lone, a way for Prince Hal to learn about the seamier side of life before assuming the mantle of King.

Of course, the McDaniel clan is not as regal as my parallel suggests. For them, stability—or at least its appearance—belongs to Gran'paw and the ancestral home at Black Mountain, rather than their present condition in Harmon. Just as Harmon does not imply "harmony," the world of Black Mountain is hardly the Lost Paradise the McDaniels imagine it to be. Cassie's songs—"Black Mountain, Black Mountain/We're a-comin', Black Mountain" and "Power in the Blood"—take on the force of choral refrain. Lone's father (a lovable drunk called Coot) hopes that "Someday, maybe, we'll all be back in the Cove, all of us with my daddy and grow things agin and love the mountains and ever'thing be right" (p. 84). However, Lone and Cassie had tried the fateful trip some twelve years earlier, and the only tangible result was a stiff dose of rheumatic fever.

Black Mountain, then, is both symbol and harsh reality. The guilts which permeate *Cassandra Singing* have their genesis there. For example, Lone's Oedipal difficulties are doubled in Coot's memory of unwitting matricide:

> "She—you know how she [Coot's mother] died, honey?" Each telling as if for the first time. "They run electric wires into the Cove when you was just a dishrag in heaven. She warshed her long, silky ha'r. Good ol' mountain-made soap. Come all the way down to her ankles like a waterfall of silver. And her with only a raggedy lavender slip on and standin' in a pool of water in the kitchen. I know he [Coot's father] blames *me*. And him sittin' there so small, an' her silver ha'r clingin' wet to ankles and around her tiny ears, and smilin' at me. Then he whispered, 'Go fetch the new ha'r-drier' we bought in Whitesburg. Me, I was thrilled 'cause it was from me *and* Daddy to her on her birthday. I handed it to her and went and put the plug in, so excited I nearly wet my pants, even if I was mor'n thirteen years old, and then ever'thing got real still and I heard my heart a-thompin' and that little click sound, like somebody suckin' at a holler tooth, and the first thing I saw was a flash like lightnin' ballin' through the room, and the shock of it hit her weak heart." (pp. 83-84)

The guilt banishes Coot from Black Mountain, but all too often the burdens of that guilt are projected from father to son. As children Lone and Cassie had tracked toward Black Mountain in an October snow. Cassie—still crippled by the experience—remembers *"That long walk in the October snow twelve years ago. Only as far as Coxton before Kyle* [her cousin] *pulled off the highway in a patrol car in front of them as said, 'That ain't the road to heaven, honey' "* (p. 28) On the other hand, Lone dreams of a return to Black Mountain via motorcycle which would obliterate Time and reconstitute primordial fathers and sons:

> Over the highway he would wind, and off the highway onto a dirt road, and somebody would tell him the way to Ishmael McDaniel's place, and he would park under a blighted chestnut tree and climb a steep path beside a stream up the deepest hollow in the mountain and, with the morning shadows still on the hillsides, see a thin ribbon of blue smoke and frost on the window, the crystals still hard. It would be

like Coot coming home after all those ruined years, and, with one strong embrace, Lone would be back in the time before the first railroad forced its way into eastern Kentucky, the first mine shaft penetrated the earth, the first macadam led the way out of the thousands of hollows into the towns. (p. 30)

Lone recovered from the rheumatic fever of his first attempt to reach Black Mountain, but the spiritual scars are still Oedipally fresh:

> "Lone," said Momma, in a loud whisper, "it's God's commandment a son love and honor his Daddy."
>
> "I wish to God he'd give me cause. He tries to forget the way he acted towards me when Cassie and me *both* laid sick in that bed. . . callin' me a sissie and a coward, sayin' I wasn't no credit to him, and me so weak with the rheumatic fever I couldn't see light. Didn't I feel low enough it was me took Cassie out in that snow and. . ."
>
> "When in this world are you going to stop blamin' yourself?" (p. 25)

Add an over-protective mother and an overly seductive sister and the Freudian mix looks just about right. In fact, some of the scenes in *Cassandra Singing* read like Lawrence's *Sons And Lovers* transplanted to Eastern Kentucky:

> "What you say, boy? You say somethin' to your father?" Lone stared into Coot's eyes. "Take them hands out your pockets and answer me, you no'count little hoodlum!"
>
> "All right, you damned malingering drunk! You stop tormentin' me, you stop throwin' off on Momma, and you clean up your nasty mess, or I'll knock the livin' hell out of you!"
>
> Drawing back his fist, Lone flinched even before Coot lashed out and the cornhusker slashed his cheek.
>
> Lone shoved him against the table, and Coot rolled off with the gun, the ironing board dropped, and the iron slid down on top of him. Lying on the floor, Coot groped for the gun and raised the muzzle. Confused by his own action, he waved the muzzle awkwardly up and down, trying to pretend he hadn't aimed it at all.
>
> "Were—you about to—*point* that thing at me?"

"Git out of this house — Git out!" (pp. 27-28)

However, Coot—like Walter Morel before him—shrinks out of the novel's central action, in his case to an attic filled with moonshine and assorted junk from Black Mountian. Cassie, Lone's "perfect twin," remains stationary and sexually troubling. Early in the novel Lone tells her to "keep that damn nightgown up over your shoulder! You ain't no little girl no more!" (p. 15). Later he warns Boyd about "touching his sister." But Kyle— two-fisted lawman and symbolic superego—calls the latently inces- tuous shot:

> "And I don't want one squeak out a *you*." Kyle shot out his arm, pointing at her. "Sleepin' with your own brother! You ain't kids no more."

> "Shut up, Kyle, by God! She was sleepin' at the foot of the cot. She was scared to sleep on that mattress or in Momma's room by herself." Kyle's holster was still empty.

> "I ought to put *her* in the reform school, too. She was hug- ged up to your back like a Siamese twin." (p. 156)

Lone's sexual difficulties are compounded by Boyd's some- time partner and female counterpart — Gypsy, who plays Clara to Cassie's Miriam in this transplanted version of Lawrentian hang-ups. Cassie and Lone are associated with the V-shaped per- simmon trees (Cassie calls them "two trunks feedin' off one set of roots") in which Lone parks his phallic motorcycle. Gypsy's sign is the X she scrawls on Lone's boot when they are to have a late night tryst at the coal silo. Lone insists that Gypsy "swear Boyd never touched you" (p. 71), but, even then, he is a reluc- tant lover at best:

> Her hand caught him between his legs and she tried to make it go in. He wanted to, but he didn't help her. He wanted to plug her mouth with his tongue, to stop her saying things that scalded his cheeks, but he could not leave her breast.

> A while later, they lay side by side, not touching. He smelled the sour damp straw that lay against the wall of the silo. She breathed deeply, sucking up jerking sighs. His head throbbed painfully. He wanted to ask Boyd to forgive him. (p. 73)

At one point Lone resists Gypsy's advances by claiming

that "Boyd might bust in on us" (p. 179), although his impotence has more to do with Cassie than a coitus-interrupting Boyd. Lone— or "Saint Lone" as Boyd and Kyle christen him on separate occasions—cannot deal with Gypsy's sexuality until he can confront the assorted guilts he feels about his sister. When Cassie, too, becomes Gypsy-like in appearance—thereby swapping vicarious experience for real living—Lone wonders if

> . . . she had really changed? Was there something in her now that responded to the makeup and the outfit, or were those trappings a way of stirring up a change she desired? No, she was ignorant. She'd heard about lovemaking and she'd read about it, no doubt, but dressing up and putting on lipstick was just disguise so they would let her into the damned world. She didn't know what sex was. Not in her blood. A lack of feeling for it? If what he had heard was true, that sometimes such energy gets drained off somewhere else, then Cassie, he hoped, was dry. But what hurt was that he couldn't be certain. It was horrible, he suddenly realized to *want* your sister to be that way: hollow inside like a lissome statue, with a smooth place, like marble, between her legs. (p. 240)

Because Cassie's childhood bout with rheumatic fever left her a cripple, Lone had lived for them both, expiating the guilt by feeding her imaginative needs. As Cassie put it: "I got ways of gettin' out without liftin' a bone" (p. 49). Some are supplied by a guitar and folk songs, others by "stacks of boxes stuffed with magazines and papers on each side of the bed against the wall. Her library of scraps" (p. 49), but most were provided by Lone himself. As Cassie says: "I've got nothin' about myself to tell anybody" (p. 123). Therefore, through much of the novel she vacillates between a desire to "live way back in the time when they built those temples in Mexico and cut your heart out on the altar" (p. 50) and the life-style she associates with Lone:

> . . . be free and not think about anything, forget ever'thing, not give a-damn for nothin'. Not to have to be somebody that's made up on ever'thing and ever'body I ever heard of or knew. Out a this bed, outsyonder in the streets of Harmon, livin' my own life and nobody else's. (p. 50)

Interestingly, Lone suffers from much the same sort of entrapment. Boyd Weaver is not only his demonic guru into the Codes of motorcycle life, but the surrogate father who might well see his bouts with Gypsy as an Oedipal invasion. If Lone is the Christ-like saint, a Grail Knight in the wasteland of Eastern Kentucky, Boyd fulfills the role of Judas. When he asks Lone if he ever found out "who it was sicked the cops" (p. 270), the answer was clear, all too clear. Lone's resulting trouble (he languishes in jail through the novel's middle section) provides Boyd with all the opportunity a Satanic figure needs. Earlier Gypsy had claimed that "You two (Boyd and Lone) set a good example for Cain and Abel" (p. 65). In fact, they are "third cousins" (p. 51); in allegorical terms, they represent the tension between would-be sainthood and hardened devildom; but that they finally become "brothers" is Freudian shorthand. As Boyd says: "At first, Charlotte (Lone's mother) just treated me like a son, for I *am* your big brother" (p. 272) Lone's sexual paralysis is a mirror image of Cassie's more pronounced passivity about life itself. And ironically, Boyd, rather than Lone, becomes the better catalyst:

> I [Boyd] want to see her git well and give her some kind of life out in the open, even if I have to play like she's just a kid that craves ridin'. It could a been *you* takin' her for her first ride. It ain't that she didn't beg. . . . I'd even go to work for that girl. Somebody's got to protect her from bastards like *me* and saints like you. (p. 272)

Boyd's family makes for a less complicated rebellion. The Weaver's dirty linen has *always* been on the public lines. Boyd has no family honor to defend, no innocence that must be stripped away. Instead, he embraces evil as his destiny. Lone, on the other hand, is virtually surrounded by what Saul Bellow has called "Reality Instructors." Diametrically opposed to the earthy permanence of Black Mountain and Ishmael McDaniel is Lone's maternal "Gran'daddy"—Corbin Stonecipher. He is the high priest of junkyards, minister to the wasteland that Harmon has become. Stonecipher's world is a graveyard of wrecked automobiles, one he controls with an apocalyptic crane and self-styled sermons on mutability:

> "Someday I'll junk this whole town. And you with it, trash of the family that you are". . .
>
> He seized Lone's hand and swung him around behind the stack of batteries. As Lone opened his mouth to curse him, the Buick's gas tank exploded. Flames shooshed up, curled above the stack. A vomit of black smoke thinned around the neck of the crane. . .
>
> ". . . like salvation, son. A way. A way to see. And seein' will

do it. See man in the muck, then see Christ on Calvary. I drop 'em
just right to get that. I want 'em to burn, to show anybody standin'
around how it ought to end.   .   .   . Right *by'er's* my altar.   .   .—and
all around here is my burnt offerin'." (p. 106-107)

The tableau is reminiscent of Fitzgerald's Valley of Ashes in *The
Great Gatsby*, although in *Cassandra Singing* the giant eyes of an
optometrist are replaced by "letters six feet tall" which proclaim:
WORK, THINK, BUY COAL (p. 110).

Stonecipher's junkyard is a vision of hell, but even its literal
flames are no match for the psychological undergrounds projected
by Uncle Virgil, evangelist of the airwaves. At first glance his
message seems predictable, full of present witness and former
"sinnin' ":

Now all I know about religion is what I know personally. And I know
I was once the most filthy-mouthed man in Harmon. Fightin', women,
and whiskey was all I knew. I used to raise hell outside every tent
meetin' I come across—poking fun. But I tell you, honey, you cain't
fool with the Lord. Them that's loudest in blasphemy, oftentimes
ends up loudest in givin' testimony. (p. 143)

However, his "sermon" to Saint Lone strikes a very different key,
one as potentially liberating as it is perplexing. One's quest is to
"Create harmony in the middle of hell" (p. 143), something he
imagines Virgil has already done. But, like Boyd before him, Virgil
is a guide through yet another avatar of hell:

But what if the hell stays right inside you? Lone, a man's lucky to
love *one* person before he dies: himself. That's only human. But the
real miracle comes when he can love his neighbor as himself. Christ
loved all men—He could do it because He was God. That's what it
takes. Maybe to love *two* persons more than yourself is blasphemy.
The saints didn't love the multitudes. They loved Jesus and for *His*
sake they *served* the multitudes. (p. 143)

Virgil follows this bit of Reality Instruction with "one last sermon,
shortest ever preached"—his suicide.

Perhaps Charlotte is right when she characterizes Lone's
problem as one of competing pressures:

No wonder he turned to trouble. Ever since he could walk, he's been
pushed and pulled ever' which way. His daddy hung over him with all

that talk of Black Mountain and farmin', and then me—Virgil—held
religion over him. And, Boyd, you and Cassie was another pull. You
tempted him into that motorsickle foolishness, and Cassie pushed him
into it with the way she acted about it. Half the thrill was tellin' *her*.
(p. 185)

Lone recovers in a burst of symbolic gesture. The bed which had
been both Cassie's prison and sanctuary now threatens to become
the prison bunk Lone will sleep in at the state reformatory. And
Cassie—"tired to death of just *witnessin'* people's misery" (p. 205)—
all too willingly offers an exchange of roles:

Lone, I tried! I tried! I pretended as long as I could. I played like we
was little again. But, Lone, I ain't no little girl no more. *I* know it, if
you don't. . . . I'll be here in Harmon the way you were. I mean, I'll
go uptown and I'll see interesting things by the truckload, and soon
I'm gonna get work. I'll come home at night and tell it all in a letter,
airmailed to La Grange [the reformatory] , describe it just so clear as
you used to tell things to me. . . . It's like we been playin' hide-and-
go-seek all our life and that bed in our room was home-free. Play like
your bunk at La Grange is our big brass bed. *Some*body's got to be *it*.
(pp. 204-206)

Earlier in the novel Lone had felt a voyeuristic attraction to the
passive life represented by Cassie's magazines and the quasi-fiction
she scribbled in their margins:

Looking at her, he wanted to stroke the sharp, aching bones of her
shoulders with his fingertips. The odd way she moved her hand as she
wrote and slid one foot down and up slightly under the quilt made
Lone wonder whether she was aware that he knelt outside. The strange
thrill of spying that he had felt many times before but had not understood until today made his heart beat even faster. Cassie spent her life
looking out on Harmon through their bedroom window, and now Lone
was on the other side of that keyhole, looking in. A good view, a view
that forced him to his knees. (p. 112)

Of course, Lone's posture is also one of prayer, appropriate to
"Saint Lone" and the shrine of Cassie's art. Haunted by Virgil and a
possible term in prison, Lone's psyche needs more forward motion
than a mere change of roles will provide. He tears the strings from
Cassie's guitar—thereby freeing himself from the prophecy of her
songs (p. 206)—and some twenty pages later Cassie burns her
magazines, opting for the open road rather than the stuff of
National Geographic. Even Black Mountain is within reach, as Lone

completed (albeit ambiguously) the long journey which has separated father and son:

> "I'm [Lone] gonna tell you somethin' that nobody, not even Cassie, knows." Lone wanted to give him something. "I have been to see Gran'paw McDaniel.".   . "Hit was just you and him—in the Cove? Did he mention my name? What did he say about me? What did you tell him?"
>
> Lone was trying to see it, to imagine how it was and what it meant to Coot.   .   . "It was just like you always told it, Coot. But he's gittin' old, and the farm's goin' down. He needs help".   .   .
>
> "Did you ask him if he forgive me, Lone?"
>
> "Well, now I tell you, Coot, he told me to tell you that—"
>
> "Don't lie".   .   .
>
> "Let me finish tellin' you," said Lone, finishing the lie that welled up in him at the prospect of what it might do to Coot. Well, it wouldn't make a new man of him—nothing would do that as completely as whiskey.   .   ."He said, 'You tell David, I've overcome my hardness toward him and that I forgive him.' " (pp. 214-215)

It is a saving lie, one filled with Conradian echoes. Yet, the "forgiveness" works in at least two directions, for Coot is both Oedipal son and Oedipal father.

If a grand illusion is effective therapy for Coot, Lone requires stronger medicine. Apparently, nothing less than the terrible truth will do. With all the suddenness of *deus ex machina* tampering, Judge Gentry suspends Lone's sentence and the repentant sinner is freed. However, Lone still has some bitter pills to swallow. When Coot presses his advantage of new-found forgiveness on Black Mountian (evidently saving lies require a good deal of re-affirmation), Lone wonders if *"a lie is the only thing I can give him?"* (p. 262) Coot is spared such anguish: *he* tells the truth, no matter how hidden or painful it might be:

> "You just don't know, Lone." He sounded almost sober. "You *never* knowed. I should a knowed it when she caught me lookin' up her dress at the Gold Sun Cafe and gave me that look. Listen, I took that woman up the mountain to the Cove, where God started when he *made* the world. But no, but no, she had to have mor'n nasty ol'

beauty all around her, had to have soot and *ce*ment and—And even when she runned off, didn't I take her back?. . . And you didn't know you had a brother, did you. I named it after me to show her I forgive her. But the Lord brought down on your Momma the punishment he saves for women like her. Then *you* come; you was the new start. But. . . she turned black as soot as the years trudged by. . . Now, Lone, you tell me what kind of a mother would lay down on that bed and fuck Boyd Weaver?. . . He [Boyd] delivered me some bottle whiskey up in the attic where I'uz finishin' this jar a rotgut, and he said, 'Keep your money, your wife's done paid for it in trade.' " (pp. 263-264)

And as the distance between Madonna and Prostitute begins to shrink—at one point he sees "Momma's guilt in Cassie's eyes" (p. 281)—Lone rejects both Cassie's interpretation of Virgil's suicide and her sexual advances. Earlier Lone had been stripped and symbolically crucified in a scene which dovetails Boyd's masochism and latent homosexuality. Ostensibly, the issue is Lone's quest for purity and its effects on Cassie. However, as he struggles against Boyd's tightening scarf, Lone learns that the monsters we hunt lurk inside. For all its trappings of castration and Black Mass, what Lone experiences is a rite of passage into the Self:

"Don't you know anything about *you*? Are *you* so pure? God, everlovin' God *damn* it! Ain't none of it *your* fault? That's right, disown her, disown all your sins! She wants to be like you were, and I'm gonna help her, and I'll hate ever' move that reminds me of you, but I will, just to be *with* her. But don't every forget—*you started it*. I'm guilty. That's it. Keep pullin' at that knot. Break loose and run—run from filth like me!. . . . You need some way for ever'body to see the difference between you and me. This'll show you how lily-white you are." Boyd scooped up snow and coal dust and threw them against Lone's chest. He scraped a huge handful off the seat of his 'cycle and dumped it over Lone's head. . . . Blinded by dust and snow, Lone heard a loud pop and a long hiss and felt cold beer on his head, running down his back and his chest. "I christen you Saint Lone, loved by all!".

"But if I was a statue, I wouldn't want to stand around with my pecker hanging out. I'd want some little boy to come along and chisel the son-of-a-bitch off."

Boyd's cold, gloved hand fumbled around Lone's groin and grabbed his penis viciously. At the touch of the blade against his skin, Lone shuddered throughout his body and screamed and raked his fingernails into the knot behind his head. (pp. 275-276)

Naked and symbolically castrated, Lone passes the test, choosing forgiveness rather than revenge, love instead of hate. Virgil's last desperate cry had been to him and only his life can give it meaning. As he puts it:

> *I'm* not gonna die! You want me to die, Cassie? You want me to die, don't you? Say it. I *know* it! But I ain't gonna kill myself, *no*body has to kill himself. Boyd stripped me down tonight, like just bein' naked would be enough to kill me. (p. 283)

Cassie and Lone end the novel in the child-like innocence of sleep, finally able to confront each other's nakedness without shame or incestuous longing. As Madden knows, there is, indeed, a "Power in the Blood." For all the loose threads and somewhat unconvincing resolution, there is a power in *Cassandra Singing* as well.

Notes

1   David Madden, *The Poetic Image in 6 Genres* (Carbondale: Southern Illinois University Press, 1969), pp. 182-183.

2   David Madden, *Cassandra Singing* (New York: Avon, 1969), p. 7. Subsequent references to *Cassandra Singing* are to this edition and pagination is given parenthetically.

VIII

Isaac Bashevis Singer and Joyce Carol Oates:

Some Versions of Gothic

There was a time in America when fiction writers were expected to be hard-drinking, tough guy types who talked about Art as if it were fishing or a bullfight, a wild party or a heavyweight boxing match. That was their special inheritance from the likes of Hemingway, Fitzgerald, and Faulkner and it set them apart (at least in the public mind) from pale, unworldly poets. Such easy distinctions could not help but make for more exceptions than instances of the rule. Names like Wallace Stevens or William Carlos Williams came to mind immediately. And in our time, James Dickey's *Deliverance* has proven that a "poet" can write a two-fisted novel with the best of them. Only Norman Mailer remains, stubbornly true to the archetype and all it implies.

I offer this thumbnail sketch, not for its originality but rather as a model for the post-Modern temper. The contemporary writer no longer gazes at *The Magic Mountain* or *Ulysses* and joins Prufrock in a chorus of "How should *I* then presume?/And how should *I* begin?" Instead, he is happy enough that the mopping up is over. The old kings are finally dead. And the new ones rule the gamut from the absurd to the zany. No doubt the frantic attempt of post-Modernists to out antiart each other is a predictable, even necessary, response. But it is not the only one. In writers as seemingly different as Isaac Bashevis Singer and Joyce Carol Oates, we see the problem from the other side of the coin. Rather than push the borders of fiction ever forward, they come at Modernism from some thoroughly old-fashioned angles. By now Singer's ongoing war against Modernism is well known. His slaps against James Joyce in particular and Modernist poets in general have a way of bringing solace to the weary English major and embarrassment to his professor. On the other hand, Miss Oates simply "writes"—with no apparent interest in literary barometers, past, present, or future.

Granted, the sort of comparative study I am suggesting sounds as if a happy marriage of oranges and apples had been arranged. In their respective modes each is a literary phenomenon, but neither the lives nor the work seems to have much in common. After all, Singer (who is seventy-plus) not only writes in Yiddish but, more importantly, he locates much of his fiction in the unfamiliar surroundings of an East European *shtetl*. He has published seven novels (three triple deckers: *The Family Moskat*, *The Manor*, and *The Estate*; and four slimmer, tighter ones: *Satan In Goray*, *The Magician Of Lublin*, *The Slave*, and *Enemies, A Love Story*, seven collections of short fiction (*Gimpel the Fool*, *The Spinoza of Market Street*, *Short Friday*, *The Seance*, *A Friend of Kafka*, *A Crown of Feathers* and *Passions*) and some seven volumes of children's fiction (*The Fearsome Inn*, *Mazel and Schlimazel*, *When Schlemiel Went To Warsaw*, *Zlateh the Goat*, *The Topsy Turvy Emperor of China*, *Joseph and Koza* and *A Day of Pleasure*). Success may have come late—from 1935 (when Singer emigrated from Poland to New York City) until 1953 he was simply another obscure, unappreciated free-lance writer for the *Jewish Daily Forward*—but the publication of "Gimpel the Fool" changed everything. What had been unthinkable for a Yiddish writer in America had, in Singer's case, come all too true. Academic criticism of his work mushroomed, along with invitations to lecture at universities and publish his fiction in magazines like *Esquire*, *Playboy* and the *New Yorker*. Cynthia Ozick's fictionalized account—"Envy, or Yiddish in America"—only tells part of the incredible story.

Several years ago, at a time when I. B. Singer's peculiar brand of dybbuks and devils was being introduced to American readers, one critic suggested playfully that "By all the laws of literary logic the work of Isaac Bashevis Singer should not exist. . ."[1] The same thing might be said of Joyce Carol Oates. She seems more a conglomerate than an individual, at least to those of us who struggle manfully against the typewriter and refuse to believe that a thirty-five-year-old author could produce five novels (*A Garden Of Earthly Delights*, *With Shuddering Fall*, *Expensive People*, *them*, and *Wonderland*), four collections of short stories (*By The North Gate*, *Upon The Sweeping Flood*, *The Wheel Of Love*, and *Marriage And Infidelities*), three volumes of poetry (*Anonymous Sins*, *Love and Its Derangements*, and *Angel Fire*), and a collection of critical essays (*The Edge Of Impossibility: Tragic Forms in Literature*)—all written in the decade between 1963 and 1973.[2]   Her stories are everywhere—in academic quarterlies and *Esquire*, in *Partisan Review* as well as *Mademoiselle*. And as each new volume appears, it is dutifully praised and her literary awards are dutifully recited. The ritual is frequent and, by now, predictable. Like I. B. Singer, she is constantly being reintroduced and always on the same tiresome terms. But interestingly enough, academic critics tend to shy away from prolonged treatments of her ever-growing canon. That she is both young and prolific may be part of the problem. And yet I suspect there are other reasons as well, ones which speak to the very heart of the post-Modernist's dilemma. As David Madden has suggested:

> . . . there is nothing new, nothing avant-garde, camp, pop, absurdist about Miss Oates's stories; reading them is like reading deeply between the hieroglyphic lines of fossils found on lonely landscapes. Her stories offer no isolatable, exploitable elements on which fashion might thrive; nor is the author's personality an exploitable by-product of her work. . .
>
> It is difficult, if not foolhardy, to discuss her stories and novels as literary fabrications. If they have form, it is so submerged in "experience" as to defy analysis.[3]

Miss Oates's early fiction tended to find its setting in a mythical Eden County, one filled with gothic echoes from Faulkner and the footprints of such Southern women as Katherine Anne Porter, Eudora Welty, and Carson McCullers. Her protagonists were primitive, her themes basic; and the glint of the ritual penknife always lurked around the edges. But rural settings and impoverished workers do not necessarily a proletarian fiction make and Miss Oates's early reviewers beat a non-existent horse when they insisted that she was a John Steinbeck *redivivus*. Rather, the typical protagonist of Miss Oates's early fiction was a curious mix of the intense and the inarticulate. In "Sweet Love Remembered," for example, she is a waitress who

> . . . moved through the clamor that began about five-thirty, a discordant ringing of silver and plates, the cash register, children's uplifted voices, and traffic from the outside, aware that she hardly heard it at all, that it seemed to her she was moving through a dream—and that this fact must express itself in her face, he must notice how quiet she had grown lately, a little reserved, a little sad—and she moved through

a kind of dream, the vulgarity and the cheapness of which she saw
about her, always about her, and her own surrender to it, a sadness of
a sweet and alluring force, a tragic, inevitable surrender to the prodding
of the loud world.[4] (p. 71)

Or the injured motorcycle rider of "What Death With Love Should
Have To Do," wondering about her boy friend:

> What did he mean, what did he know? He was brutal and ignorant, at
> the end of these races he would stagger about, drinking beer, laughing,
> showing everybody the nicks and scratches on his face and hands, as
> if there were something about blood that was funny. . . . But what
> has this to do with love, Mae thought dizzily, what has blood to do
> with love and why did they go together? Why were they related?[5]
> (p. 216)

It is a world of dime stores and basic needs, of blood and birth and
death, all rendered with an empathy which is Miss Oates's special
magic. Such inner lives have a way of being unsettling, not because
we are so different from her protagonists but, rather, because we
are so close. That is why reading Miss Oates's work can be a painful
experience. Her characters are not sophisticated enough to sidetrack
the inevitable tragedies which await them. Only passion remains,
nonverbal and desperate:

> His students were desperate, doomed young people, many of them
> from the country, remote incidental rural sections of the state, bewil-
> dered at their failure (they were assigned to this course because they
> were far below average in English), unable to comprehend his teaching,
> his encouragement, his love. Their failure had widened their eyes, giving
> them the alert, electric look of animals to whom all movements signal
> danger. Like animals, they appeared mild and obedient until, knowing
> themselves trapped, they slashed out at him as if he were the crystal-
> lization of the forces that had maimed them—the obscure, mysterious
> spirit of the famous university itself so available to them (they, with
> their high-school diplomas) and yet, as it turned out, so forbidden to
> them, its great machinery even now working, perhaps, to process cards,
> grades, symbols that would send them back to their families and the
> lives they had escaped.[6] (p. 168)

"Archways" is a prototype of *them*, this time told from the perspective of a young instructor who dabbles with the possibility of
suicide and settles for mediocrity. In Miss Oates's first collection of
stories, *By The North Gate* (1963), only "The Expense of Spirit"

had gone collegiate. Since then the groves of academe have proven nearly as fertile as those ominous bushes one finds in Eden County. This is not to suggest that Miss Oates is likely to run us through yet another round of academic parties full of thinly veiled literary gossip. Her one attempt at making fictional capital from campus woes—a stab at academic bitchiness called *Hungry Ghosts* (1974)— is, happily, an exception rather than her rule. The landscapes of the heart are still supreme, although a sensitive young academic—like the Carl of "The Survival of Childhood"—can give them some new wrinkles:

> At thirty-three he was aware of, had adjusted to certain inadequacies in himself. His childhood had turned his gaze inward, limiting it, wisely, to that small sphere within which lay the potentiality of his success, and he had not been deluded, as his mother had, by mythical bonds of responsibility and selflessness that would have drained his energy, distracted his vision of himself. He had recognized as a child the terrible isolation of the self-conscious individual within a world of complex links—of relationships of blood, emotion, of economic accident; he had recognized the hollowness within these links, the illusions that sustained them.[7] (pp. 47-48)

Them is a gothic novel, one which brings many of Miss Oates's earlier themes to a rapid boil. The machinery of a Monk Lewis or a Mary Shelley has disappeared; only the effects are there, internationalized and equally terrifying. Eden County—that world where innocence and the baptism of blood live in a shaky co-existence—may owe its land grant to Faulkner, but it is Poe who hovers over the corpses. This is especially true when Miss Oates abandons the backcountry (at least temporarily) and turns, instead, to *The Wheel Of Love*. In the earlier stories, violence was a function of the omnipresent knife; later, it becomes the terrors associated with love itself. As one of the multiple protagonists of "Unmailed, Unwritten Letters" puts it:

> Let me admit the worst—anxious not to fall in love with him, I think of not loving him at the very moment he enters me. I think of him already boarding a plane and disappearing from my life, with relief, I think with pity of human beings and this sickness of theirs, this desire for unity. . . . Lying in his arms I am inspired to hurt him. I say that we will have to give this up, these meetings; too much risk, shame. What about my husband, what about his wife? (A deliberate insult—I know he doesn't love his wife.) I can see at once that I've hurt him, his face shows every-

thing, and as soon as this registers in both of us I am stunned with the
injustice of what I've done to him, I must erase it, cancel it out, undo
it; I caress his body in desperation. . . .[8] (pp. 66-67)

Stories like "Where Have You Been, Where Are You Going?" or
"Demons"—in which seduction and horror unfold simultaneously—
are designed to maximize chills and send them up a reader's spine
long into the night. It is a fiction where victim and victimizer slowly
change places and, all too often, what the heart discovers about
itself is truly frightening. The opening lines of "The Assailant" are
typical:

> There are those strange, ugly times when your body seems
> transparent, your skin draws too tight, something, so that the height-
> ened beat of the heart and the minute hissing of blood through veins
> seems a concern not just of yourself but of everyone watching you.[9]
> (p. 300)

After the twenty-odd stories of *The Wheel Of Love*, one no longer
quite believes in the banal again.

No doubt Miss Oates's work will, one day, be subjected to
the full critical arsenal: some avatar of Malcolm Cowley will provide
a map of Eden County, complete with genealogies of the Carletons
and the Reveres; psychological critics will give both Miss Oates and
her frigid protagonists the works; and the sprinkles of Catholicism
will attract the Religion & Lit. crowd. But it is the gothic element
we *feel*. And, for Miss Oates, that may be enough.

In a sense, I. B. Singer has it easier: readers approach his
fiction without the usual baggage of expectations. And, soon, that
special relationship between a storyteller and his audience is re-
established—despite the manifestoes of Modernists and post-Modernists alike. As Gimpel—formerly a "fool"—puts it:

> I wandered over the land, and good people did not neglect me.
> After many years I became old and white; I heard a great deal, many
> lies and falsehoods, but the longer I lived the more I understood that
> there are really no lies. Whatever doesn't really happen is dreamed at
> night. It happens to one if it doesn't happen to another, tomorrow if
> not today, or a century hence if not next year. What difference can
> it make? Often I heard tales of which I said, "Now this is a thing that
> cannot happen." But before a year had elapsed I heard that it actually

had come to pass somewhere.

> Going from place to place, eating at strange tables, it often happens that I spin yarns—improbable things that could never have happened—about devils, magicians, windmills and the like.[10] (pp. 312-313)

"Devils, magicians, windmills, and the like"—these are the gothic elements which come alive in the fiction of I. B. Singer, as if the flesh of the quotation were the flesh of Gimpel, but its spirit is the spirit of Singer.

But, unlike Gimpel, Singer knows that it is exactly the "improbable" which *does* happen. And the assorted imps and devils, *dybbuks* and other ghosts who populate his fiction are supernatural extensions of the general truth. As his characters learn, over and over again: "Everything is possible." Singer insists upon making careful distinctions between possibilities of the novel and those of the short story. For him, there is something about a *dybbuk* which demands shortness; such a character could not be the subject of a novel. On the other hand, there is more than a little secret sharing between Joyce Carol Oates's *With Shuddering Fall* and "What Death With Love Should Have To Do." Both partake of that violent world of motorcycle racing which kicks up the dust around Eden County. Of course, as a Yiddish writer from Eastern Europe, Singer inherits a special burden, one of proving that he, too, can write endless family sagas on the order of a Galsworthy. And it is easy to see that a *dybbuk* could not have enough prodigy to make for a *Family Moskat*.

More importantly, it is the short story which allows for the possibility of perfection. And while it may be true that all of Singer's "heroes are possessed people—possessed by a mania, by a fixed idea, by a strange kind of fear or passion,"[11] the gothic flavor is most sharply defined in the shorter fiction. At times—as in "Shiddah and Kuziba"—the supernatural world is all, but, more often, it dovetails into what we call the "real world." "Gretzel the Monkey" is a good example of the latter type. As Irving Buchen suggests:

> . . . Singer presents the notion that all men exist in two forms: in an actual form which is fixed and more or less known; and in a secret form which is unformed and more or less unknown. The former is

always specific and an original; the latter mysterious and a shadow. To Singer, a shadow is each personality's intimate dybbuk or secret sharer. Dreams, fantasies, sinful desires—all are the expressions of a shadow and represent what an individual might be if he and his shadow exchanged roles and clothes. (p. 126)

In either case, the world of Singer's fiction is a self-consciously excessive one. His "scholars"—like "The Spinoza of Market Street"—slowly become wrinkled Fausts; his lovers, both homo- and hetero-sexual, follow each other into the next world or back from it; and his women (e.g., "Henne Fire") are such a mix of demon and shrew that their tongues literally can start fires.

The hysteria factor reaches its highest pitch when Singer writes about *shochets*, or ritual slaughters. In "Blood," for example, the killing of animals is associated with sexual lust—as Singer himself suggests in the opening lines: "The cabalists know that the passion for blood and the passion for flesh have the same origin, and this is the reason 'Thou shalt not kill' is followed by 'Thou shalt not commit adultery.' " But even with all its punches telegraphed, the splendor in the slaughterhouse is chilling nonetheless:

> While the beasts were bleeding, Risha threw off her clothes and stretched out naked on a pile of straw. Reuben came to her and they were so fat their bodies could barely join. They puffed and panted. Their wheezing mixed with the deathrattles of the animals made an unearthly noise; contorted shadows fell on the walls; the shed was saturated with the heat of blood.[12] (p. 42)

And Reuben's corruption is twofold; eventually he adds the selling of non-kosher meat to his original crimes of passion. However, in "The Slaughterer," politics force Yoineh Meir to become a *shochet* and the result is hysteria of another sort:

> Yoineh Meir no longer slept at night. If he dozed off, he was immediately beset by nightmares. Cows assumed human shape, with beards and side locks, and skullcaps over their horns. Yoineh Meir would be slaughtering a calf, but it would turn into a girl. Her neck throbbed, and she pleaded to be saved. She ran to the study house and spattered the courtyard with her blood. He even dreamed that he had slaughtered Reitze Doshe instead of a sheep.
>
> In one of his nightmares, he heard a human voice come from a slaughtered goat. The goat, with his throat slit, jumped on Yoineh Meir

and tried to butt him, cursing in Hebrew and Aramatic, spitting and fuming at him. Yoineh Meir awakened in a sweat.[13] (p. 24)

Singer's most recent stories retain their attraction to the grotesque. But now his *dybbuks* tend to hang out in New York cafeterias. And, too, the distance between Singer and his *personaes* has shrunk. Gimpel was a convenient index, a way of allowing Singer to get some native ideas off his chest. The same thing is true of *The Magicians Of Lublin*: the thinly veiled autobiography (the writer-as-magician) provides Singer with a metaphorical spokesman. And when Yasha Mazur, his surrogate artist, says, "Well, everyone has something that he keeps to himself. Each person has his secrets. If the world had even been informed of what went on inside him, he, Yasha, would long ago have been committed to a madhouse," Singer and the magician become doppelgängers.

Interestingly enough, a similar speech occurs in "Guests on a Winter Night," but this time protagonist and author are the same:

> At the head of the table, my father sat in a black velvet robe beneath which a yellowish fringed garment showed. . . . I looked at him with love, and also with astonishment. Why was he my father? What would have happened if someone else had been my father? Would I have been the same Isaac? . . .

> A strange thought occurred to me—that he resembled the czar whose picture hung in our cheder. I knew well enough that a comparison like that was a sacrilege. The czar was a vicious man, and my father was pious and a rabbi. But my brain was full of crazy thoughts. If people knew what I was thinking, they would put me in prison.[14]

Singer has always been a curious blend of the cosmopolitan and the shy, as if a part of him still lived *In My Father's Court*. His mannerisms—and many of his Yiddish expressions—are those of the traditional *yeshiva bocher* (religious student). In his latest stories the narrative filter is often Singer himself, a writer forced to watch yet another world in the process of disintegration:

> As happens so often in New York, the neighborhood changed. The synagogues became churches, the yeshivas restaurants or garages. Here and there one could still see a Jewish old people's home, a shop selling Hebrew books, a meeting place for *landsleit* from some village in Roumania or Hungary. I had to come downtown a few times a week, because the Yiddish newspaper to which I contributed was still

there. In the cafeteria on the corner, in former times one could meet Yiddish writers, journalists, teachers, fund raisers for Israel, and the like. Blintzes, borscht, kreplach, chopped liver, rice pudding, and egg cookies were the standard dishes. Now the place catered mainly to Negroes and Puerto Ricans.[15]

The character of Joel Yabloner—the cabalist whom Singer later meets in the run-down cafeteria—is based upon an actual person, S. Setzer. He is one of the exotic scholars described in Herbert Weiner's *9½ Mystics*, ironically enough in a chapter entitled "A Mystic on East Broadway." Singer alters the facts—taking Yabloner to Jerusalem (where he gives lectures on the Cabala) and then back to a lonely death in New York—but it is the narrator's final questions which are the heart of the matter:

> A few weeks later, I read among the obituaries that Joel Yabloner had died. He was buried somewhere in Brooklyn. That night I lay awake until three o'clock, thinking about him. Why did he return? Had he not atoned enough for the sins of his youth? Had his return to East Broadway some explanation in the lore of the cabala? Had some holy sparks strayed from the World of Emanation into the Evil Host? And could they have been found and brought back to their sacred origin only in this cafeteria? Another idea came into my head—perhaps he wanted to lie near that teacher with whom he exchanged eyeglasses? I remembered the last words I heard from him: "Man does not live according to reason." (p. 142)

All the essential elements of a Singer story are there: the possessed character, the questioning protagonist, the figures in the cabalistic carpet,—but, somehow, it falls flat, as if Singer were insisting too much upon his own aesthetic principles.

On the other hand, "The Third One" is an example of Singer's narrative filter at its best. Once again a New York —the sort that Singer used to haunt as a free-lance writer for Yiddish publications—provides the setting. The story itself is an *objet touvé*, one thrust upon the reluctant narrator. It involves the marital triangle of Fingerbein, his wife, and her switch-hitting *hausfreund*. Singer doubles as non-directive therapist—allowing Fingerbein to tell his story without interruption—and professional writer. After all, as Fingerbein puts it:

> "You write about religion, marriage, and sex, and I often admire how well you understand modern man, with his complexities and pit-

falls. But all you can do is criticize—you can't show the way back to faith. It's impossible for us to conduct ourselves like our parents and grandparents without having their piety. I will tell you something, though I'm ashamed to admit it. . . perhaps I should return to God." I took out the tractate of Betzah, opened it, and began to hum as in the old times. "If an egg was laid on festival day, the school of Shammai say: It may be eaten. And the school of Hillel say: It may not be eaten." I kept nodding and humming like a yeshiva boy for a good half hour. In the beginning, it was nostalgically sweet, but the more I went on the heavier the spirit felt. As long as one believed that these laws were given to Moses on Mount Sinai, there was meaning. Without this faith, it's all sheer scholasticism.[16] (p. 221)

But the tension is not, finally, between Singer and Fingerbein or between Fingerbein and his unorthodox family. Rather, it is an interior quarrel, one which pits aspects of Singer against each other. The compulsions have, at last, come full-circle. Would-be rabbi and Yiddish writer merge—and both the writer and his story strike us as true.

Ours is a time characterized by endless talk about the death of the novel and other linear casualties. As Leslie Fiedler so gleefully puts it:

> We have, however, entered into quite another time—apocalyptic, anti-rational, blatantly romantic and sentimental; an age dedicated to joyous misology and prophetic irresponsibility; one distrustful of self-protective irony and too-great self-awareness. . . . He [i.e., John Lennon] thus provides one more model for the young who, without any special gift or calling, in the name of mere possibility, insist on making tens of thousands of records, movies, collections of verse, paintings, junk sculptures, even novels in complete contempt of professional standards.[17] (p. 462)

Of course, there are other literary weathermen rushing to bring us the "good news" about pop-up novels or random poetry, but it is Fiedler who always seems to raise the finger first. And yet, while champions of the "thin novel"—like Kurt Vonnegut or Richard Brautigan—may become the fashionable yardsticks, I suspect there will always be those who prefer the darkly serious fiction of Joyce Carol Oates and Isaac Bashevis Singer. Theirs is a commitment to the power of the imagination which must wait for the individual reader to open their work and begin: "I was in love with a man I couldn't marry, so one of us had to die—I lay awake, my eyes twitching in the dark, trying to understand which one of us should die."

Notes

1   Irving Buchen, *Isaac Bashevis Singer and the Eternal Past* (New York: New York University Press, 1968), p. 197. Subsequent references to Professor Buchen are to this book and pagination is included parenthetically.

2   Since 1973 her productivity has, if anything, only increased. Novels, collections of short fiction, critical essays, book reviews, poetry and plays threaten to make her work a three-foot shelf all its own.

3   David Madden, *The Poetic Image in 6 Genres* (Carbondale: Southern Illinois University Press, 1969), p. 27.

4   Joyce Carol Oates, "Sweet Love Remembered" in *By the North Gate* (New York: Vanguard, 1963), p. 71.

5   Joyce Carol Oates, "What Death With Love Should Have To Do" in *Upon the Sweeping Flood* (New York: Vanguard, 1966), p. 216.

6   Joyce Carol Oates, "Archways" in *Upon the Sweeping Flood* (New York: Vanguard, 1966), p. 168.

7   Joyce Carol Oates, "The Survival of Childhood" in *Upon the Sweeping Flood* (New York: Vanguard, 1966), pp. 47-48.

8   Joyce Carol Oates, "Unmailed, Unwritten Letters" in *The Wheel of Love* (New York: Vanguard,1970), pp. 66-67.

9   Joyce Carol Oates, "The Assailant" in *The Wheel of Love* (New York: Vanguard, 1970), p. 300.

10   Isaac Bashevis Singer, "Gimpel the Fool," *Partisan Review*, XX, No. 3 (May-June 1953), pp. 312-313.

11   Sanford Pinsker, "Isaac Bashevis Singer: An Interview," *Critique*, XI, No. 2, p. 22.

12   Isaac Bashevis Singer, "Blood" in *Short Friday* (New York: Signet edition, 1965), p. 42.

13   Isaac Bashevis Singer, "The Slaughterer" in *The Seance* (New York: Farrar, Straus and Giroux, 1968), p. 24.

14   Isaac Bashevis Singer, "Guests on a Winter Night" in *A Friend of Kafka* (New York: Farrar, Straus and Giroux) pp. 17-18

15 Isaac Bashevis Singer, "The Cabalist of East Broadway" in *A Crown of Feathers* (New York: Farrar, Straus and Giroux, 1973), p. 135. Subsequent references to the story are to this edition and pagination is given parenthetically.

16 Isaac Bashevis Singer, "The Third One" in *A Crown of Feathers* (New York: Farrar, Straus and Giroux, 1973), p. 221.

17 Leslie Fiedler, "Cross the Border, Close the Gap" in *Collected Essays*, II (New York: Stein & Day, 1971), p. 462.

A Selected Bibliography of the

American Novel in the 1960's

Aldrige, John. *Time to Murder and Create: The Contemporary Novel in Crisis.* New York: David McKay, 1966.

Allen, Mary. *The Necessary Blankness: Women in Major American Fiction of the Sixties.* Urbana: University of Illinois Press, 1976.

Bellamy, Joe David. *The New Fiction: Interviews with Innovative American Writers.* Urbana: University of Illinois Press. 1975.

Bryant, Jerry H. *The Open Decision: The Contemporary American Novel and its Intellectual Background.* New York: Free Press, 1970.

Fiedler, Leslie. *Waiting for the End.* New York: Stein and Day, 1964.

French, Michael R. "The American Novel in the Sixties," *Midwest Quarterly*, 9 (July 1968), 365-79.

Gass, William H. *Fiction and the Figures of Life.* New York: Knopf, 1970.

Harris, Charles B. *Contemporary American Novelists of the Absurd.* New Haven: College and University Press, 1971.

Hassan, Ihab. *Contemporary American Literature: An Introduction.* New York: Ungar, 1973.

    . *Dismemberment of Orpheus: Toward a Postmodern Literature.* New York: Oxford University Press, 1971.

    . *Paracriticisms: Seven Speculations of the Times.* Urbana: University of Illinois Press, 1975.

Kazin, Alfred. *Bright Book of Life: American Novelists & Storytellers From Hemingway to Mailer.* Boston: Little, Brown and Co., 1973.

Klinkowitz, Jerome. *Literary Disruptions: The Making of a Post-Contemporary American Fiction.* Urbana: University of Illinois Press, 1975.

Kostelanetz, Richard. *The End of Intelligent Writing: Literary Politics in America.* New York: Sheed, 1974.

Levine, Paul. "The Intemperate Zone: The Climate of Contemporary American Fiction," *Massachusetts Review*, 8 (Summer 1967), 505-23.

Lewis, R. W. B. *Trials of the Word: Essays in American Literature and the Humanistic Tradition.* New Haven: Yale University Press, 1965.

Olderman, Raymond Michael. *Beyond the Waste Land: A Study of the American Novel in the Nineteen-Sixties.* New Haven: Yale University Press, 1965.

Poirier, Richard. *Performing Self: Compositions & Decompositions in the Languages of Contemporary Life.* New York: Oxford University Press, 1971.

Scholes, Robert. *The Fabulators.* New York: Oxford University Press, 1967.

Schulz, Max F. *Black Humor Fiction of the Sixties: A Pluralistic Definition of Man and His World.* Athens: Ohio Univeristy Press, 1973.

Solotaroff, Theodore. *The Red Hot Vacuum.* New York: Atheneum, 1970.

Tanner, Tony. *City of Words.* Harper and Row, 1971.

Weinberg, Helen. *The New Novel in America: The Kafkan Mode in Contemporary Fiction.* Ithaca, N. Y.: Cornell University Press, 1970.

WORKS BY JOHN BARTH

The Floating Opera. Englewood Cliffs, N. J.: Appleton-Century-Crofts, 1956.

The End of the Road. New York: Doubleday, 1958.

The Sot-Weed Factor. New York: Doubleday, 1960.

Giles Goat-Boy. New York: Doubleday, 1966.

Lost in the Funhouse. New York: Doubleday, 1968.

Chimera. New York: Random House, 1972.

SELECTED WORKS ABOUT JOHN BARTH

Enck, John. "John Barth: An Interview," *Wisconsin Studies in Contemporary Literature,* 6 (Winter-Spring 1965), pp. 3-14.

Gross, Beverly. "The Anti-Novels of John Barth," *Chicago Review,* 20 (Nov. 1958), pp. 95-109.

Hauck, Richard Boyd. "These Fruitful Odysseys: John Barth," in *A Cheerful Nihilism: Confidence and 'The Absurd' in American Humorous Fiction.* Bloomington: Indiana University Press, 1971.

Poirier, Richard. "The Politics of Self-Parody," *Partisan Review,* 35 (Summer 1968), pp. 339-353.

Rovit, Earl. "The Novel as Parody: John Barth," *Critique,* 6 (Fall 1963), pp. 77-85

Tharpe, Jac. *John Barth: The Comic Sublimity of Paradox.* Carbondale: Southern Illinois University Press, 1974.

WORKS BY BRUCE JAY FRIEDMAN

Stern. New York: Simon and Schuster, 1962.

A Mother's Kisses. New York: Simon and Schuster, 1964.

Black Angels. New York: Simon and Schuster, 1964.

Far From the City of Class. New York: Frommer-Pasmantier, 1963.

The Dick. New York: Knopf, 1970.

About Harry Towns. New York: Knopf, 1974.

WORKS ABOUT BRUCE JAY FRIEDMAN

Kaplan, Charles, "Escape into Hell: Friedman's *Stern.*" *College English Journal,* I (1965), iii, pp. 25-30.

Lewis, Stuart. "Myth and Ritual in the Short Fiction of Bruce Jay Friedman."
    Studies in Short Fiction 10: pp. 415-416.

;chulz, Max. *Bruce Jay Friedman.* New York: Twayne, 1974.

WORKS BY JOSEPH HELLER

itch-22. New York: Simon and Schuster, 1961.

)mething Happened. New York: Knopf, 1974.

WORKS ABOUT JOSEPH HELLER

ihan, Richard and Patch, Jerry. "*Catch-22;* The Making of a Novel."
    Minnesota Review, VII (1967), pp. 238-244.

arl, Frederick R. "Joseph Hller's *Catch-22*: Only Fools Walk in Darkness."
    Contemporary American Novelists, ed. Harry T. Moore. Carbondale:
    Southern Illinois University Press, 1965, pp. 134-142.

ey, Frederick and McDonald, Walter, eds. *A Catch-22 Casebook.* New York:
    Thomas Y. Crowell, 1973.

McDonald, James L. "I See Everything Twice: The Structure of Joseph
    Heller's *Catch-22.*" *University Review,* XXXIV (1968), pp. 175-180.

Mellard, James M. "*Catch-22: Deja vu* and the Labyrinth of Memory."
    Bucknell Review, XVI, No. 2 (1968), pp. 29-44.

Nagel, James, ed. *Critical Essays on Catch-22.* Encino, Calif.: Dickenson
    Publishing Co., 1974.

Pinsker, Sanford. "Heller's *Catch-22*: The Protest of a *Puer Eternis.*" *Critique,*
    VII, No. 2 (1965), pp. 150-162.

Solomon, Jan. "The Structure of Joseph Heller's *Catch-22.*" *Critique,* IX,
    No. 2 (1967), pp. 46-57.

Waldmeir, Joseph J. "Two Novelists of the Absurd: Heller and Kesey."
    Wisconsin Studies in Contemporary Literature, V, No. 3, pp. 192-196.

WORKS BY KEN KESEY

One Flew Over the Cuckoo's Nest. New York: Viking Press, 1962.

Sometimes a Great Notion. New York: Viking Press, 1964.

Garage Sale. New York: Viking Press, 1973.

WORKS ABOUT KEN KESEY

Blessing, Richard. "Ken Kesey's Evolving Hero," *Journal of Popular Culture,* IV (Winter 1971), pp. 615-627.

Leeds, Barry H. "Theme and Technique in *One Flew Over the Cuckoo's Nest,'* *Western American Literature,* XLVI (May 1974), pp. 200-206.

Mills, Nicolaus. "Ken Kesey and the Politics of Laughter." *Centennial Review* XVI (Winter 1972), pp. 82-90.

Sherman, W. D. "The Novels of Ken Kesey." *Journal of American Studies,* (1971), pp. 185-196.

Sherwood, Terry G. *"One Flew Over the Cuckoo's Nest* and the Comic Strip *Critique,* XIII (No. 1 1970), pp. 97-109.

Zaskin, Elliot M. "Political Theorist and Demiurge: The Rise and Fall of Ke Kesey." *Centennial Review,* 17 (Spring 1973), pp. 199-213.

WORKS BY DAVID MADDEN

The Beautiful Greed. New York: Random House, 1961.

Wright Morris (criticism). New York: Twayne, 1964.

Cassandra Singing. New York: Crown, 1969.

The Poetic Image in 6 Genres. Carbondale: Southern Illinois University Press, 1969.

The Shadow Knows. Baton Rouge: University of Louisiana Press, 1970.

James M. Cain (criticism). New York: Twayne, 1970.

American Dreams, American Nightmares (criticism). Carbondale: Southern Illinois University Press, 1970.

Brothers in Confidence. New York: Avon, 1972.

Bijou. New York: Crown, 1974.

The Suicide's Wife. New York: Bobbs-Merrill, 1978.

WORKS ABOUT DAVID MADDEN

Pinsker, Sanford. "A Conversation with David Madden." *Critique,* Vol. XV, No. 2, pp. 5-15.

WORKS BY JOYCE CAROL OATES

By the North Gate. New York: Vanguard Press, 1963.

With Shuddering Fall. New York: Vanguard Press, 1964.

Upon the Sweeping Flood. New York: Vanguard Press, 1966.

Garden of Earthly Delights. New York: Vanguard Press, 1967.

Expensive People. New York: Vanguard Press, 1968.

them. New York: Vanguard Press, 1969.

The Wheel of Love. New York: Vanguard Press, 1970.

Wonderland. New York: Vanguard Press, 1971.

Marriage and Infidelities. New York: Vanguard Press, 1972.

The Edge of Impossibility (criticism). New York: Vanguard Press, 1972.

Do With Me What You Will. New York: Vanguard Press, 1973.

The Hostile Sun (criticism). Los Angeles: Black Sparrow Press, 1974.

The Hungry Ghosts. Los Angeles: Black Sparrow Press, 1974.

The Goddess & Other Women. New York: Vanguard Press, 1974.

New Heaven, New Earth (criticism). New York: Vanguard Press, 1974.

The Assassins. New York: Vanguard Press, 1975.

The Poisoned Kiss. New York: Vanguard Press, 1975.

Childwold. New York: Vanguard Press, 1976.

Son of the Morning. New York: Vanguard Press, 1978.

WORKS ABOUT JOYCE CAROL OATES

Bellamy, Joe David. "The Dark Lady of American Letters: An Interview with Joyce Carol Oates." *Atlantic*, CCXXIX (February 1972), pp. 63-67.

Kazin, Alfred. "Oates." *Harper's*, CCXLIII (August 1971), pp. 78-82.

Madden, David. "The Violent World of Joyce Carol Oates" in *The Poetic Image in 6 Genres* (Carbondale: Southern Illinois University Press, 1969), pp. 25-47.

Pickering, Samuel F., Jr. "The Short Stories of Joyce Carol Oates." *Georgia Review*, XXVIII (Summer 1974), pp. 218-226.

Taylor, Gordon O. "Joyce Carol Oates, Artist in Wonderland." *Southern Review*, X (Spring 1974), pp. 490-503.

Sullivan, Walter. "The Artificial Demon: Joyce Carol Oates and the Dimensions of the Real." *Hollins Critic*, IX (December 1972), pp. 1-12.

WORKS BY PHILIP ROTH

Goodbye, Columbus. Boston: Houghton Mifflin, 1967.

Letting Go. New York: Random House, 1961.

When She Was Good. New York: Random House, 1966.

Portnoy's Complaint. New York: Random House, 1967.

)ur Gang. New York: Random House, 1971.

The Breast. New York: Holt, Rinehart and Winston, 1972.

'be Great American Novel. New York: Holt, Rinehart and Winston, 1973.

My Life as a Man. New York: Holt, Rinehart and Winston, 1974.

Reading Myself and Others. New York: Farrar, Straus and Giroux, 1975.

The Professor of Desire. New York: Farrar, Straus and Giroux, 1977.

WORKS ABOUT PHILIP ROTH

Howe, Irving. "Philip Roth, Reconsidered," *Commentary,* 54 (December 1972), pp. 69-77.

McDaniel, John N. *The Fiction of Philip Roth.* Haddonfield, N. J.: Haddonfield House, 1974.

Pinsker, Sanford. *The Comedy that "Hoits": An Essay on the Fiction of Philip Roth.* Columbia, Mo.: University of Missouri Press, 1975.

Solotaroff, Theodore. "Philip Roth and the Jewish Moralists," *Chicago Review,* 13 (Winter 1959), pp. 87-99.

WORKS BY ISAAC BASHEVIS SINGER

Satan in Goray. New York: Farrar, Straus and Giroux, 1955.

Gimpel the Fool. New York: Farrar, Straus and Giroux, 1957.

The Magician of Lublin. New York: Farrar, Straus and Giroux, 1960.

The Spinoza of Market Street. New York: Farrar, Straus and Giroux, 1961.

The Slave. New York: Farrar, Straus and Giroux, 1962.

Short Friday. New York: Farrar, Straus and Giroux, 1964.

The Family Moskat. New York: Farrar, Straus and Giroux, 1965.

In My Father's Court (memoirs). New York: Farrar, Straus and Giroux, 196(

The Manor. New York: Farrar, Straus and Giroux, 1967.

The Seance. New York: Farrar, Straus and Giroux, 1968.

The Estate. New York: Farrar, Straus and Giroux, 1969.

A Friend of Kafka. New York: Farrar, Straus and Giroux, 1970.

Enemies, a Love Story. New York: Farrar, Straus and Giroux, 1972.

A Crown of Feathers. New York: Farrar, Straus and Giroux, 1973.

Passions. New York: Farrar, Straus and Giroux, 1975.

Shosha. New York: Farrar, Straus and Giroux, 1978.

WORKS ABOUT ISAAC BASHEVIS SINGER

Allentuck, Marcia, ed. *The Achievement of Isaac Bashevis Singer.* Carbonda
Southern Illinois University Press, 1969.

Buchen, Irving H. *Isaac Bashevis Singer and the Eternal Past.* New Yoi
New York University Press, 1968.

Fixler, Michael. "The Redeemers: Themes in the Fiction of Isaac Bashe\
Singer." *Kenyon Review*, XXVI (Spring 1964), pp. 371-386.

Howe, Irving. "I. B. Singer." *Encounter*, XXVI (March 1966), pp. 60-7

Malin, Irving, ed. *Critical Views of Isaac Bashevis Singer.* New York: Ne
York University Press, 1969.

Pinsker, Sanford. "The Fictive Worlds of Isaac Bashevis Singer." *Critiq
XI (No. 2, 1969), pp. 26-39.

Siegel, Ben. *Isaac Bashevis Singer.* Minneapolis: University of Minne
Press. 1969.

Wolkenfield, J. S.   "Isaac Bashevis Singer: The Faith of his Devils and
    Magicians." *Criticism,* V (Fall 1963), pp. 349-359.

Zatlin, Linda G.   "The Themes of Isaac Bashevis Singer's Short Fiction,"
    Critique, XI (No. 2, 1969), pp. 40-46.

                        WORKS BY KURT VONNEGUT, JR.

Player Piano. New York: Charles Scribner's Sons, 1952.

The Sirens of Titan. Boston: Houghton-Mifflin, 1961.

Mother Night. Greenwich, Conn.: Fawcett, 1961 (printed February, 1962).

Cat's Cradle. New York: Holt, Rinehart & Winston, 1963.

God Bless You, Mr. Rosewater. New York: Holt, Rinehart & Winston, 1965.

Slaughterhouse-Five. New York: Delacorte/Seymour Lawrence, 1969.

Breakfast of Champions. New York: Delacorte/Seymour Lawrence, 1973.

Wampeters, Foma, & Granfalloons: Opinions (essays). New York: Delacorte/
    Seymour Lawrence, 1974.

Slap-Stick. New York: Delacorte/Seymour Lawrence, 1976.

                        WORKS ABOUT KURT VONNEGUT, JR.

Fiedler, Leslie A.   "The Divine Stupidity of Kurt Vonnegut." *Esquire,* 74
    (September 1970), pp. 195-197, 199-200, 202-204.

Goldsmith, David. *Kurt Vonnegut: Fantasist of Fire and Ice* (Popular Writers
    Series Pamphlet No. 2). Bowling Green, Ohio: Bowling Green Univer-
    sity Popular Press, 1972.

Greiner, Donald L. "Vonnegut's Slaughterhouse-Five and the Fiction of
    Atrocity." *Critique,* 14, No. 3 (1973), pp. 38-51.

Klinkowitz, Jerome and John Somer, eds. *The Vonnegut Statement.* New York: Delacorte/Seymour Lawrence, 1973.

Reed, Peter. *Kurt Vonnegut* (Writers for the Seventies Series). New York: Warner Books, 1972.